Learning to Choose

Discover Learning Lessons From The Seven Choices an Aspiring Creative Entrepreneur Made to Reach His Hidden Potential

Evan Snow

Copyright © 2023 by Evan Snow

All rights reserved

Table of Contents

Prologue: What I Want You To Know 1

Chapter 1: Childhood (I Was The Bad Kid In School) 7

Chapter 2: The 7 Moments That Changed My Life 17

Chapter 3: Learning To Choose: Art, Culture, And House Music ... 21

Chapter 4: Learning To Choose The "Aha Moment" 35

Chapter 5: Learning To Choose Psilocybin And Boiler Room 48

Chapter 6: Learning To Choose A Business Partner 69

Chapter 7: Learning To Choose A Venture (Art Fort Lauderdale - "The Art Fair On The Water") 81

Chapter 8: Learning To Choose Yoga During COVID 97

Chapter 9: Learning To Choose Not Giving Up 110

Chapter 10: Learning To Choose Helping Others 117

Chapter 11: Learning To Choose Men's Work And Self-Care 124

Some Recommendations To Help Improve Your Life Even More ... 135

Prologue

What I Want You To Know

"Everything Happens For A Reason, The Good And The Bad"
- Evan Snow

The road will not be easy; in fact, it can be quite hard. But I am here to tell you with the utmost sincerity, you can do it. You can be who you want to be. You can craft the life you want to live, against all odds.

I'm not entirely sure why, but a few years ago I reached a pivotal shift in my life that led me to making the first of many decisions. I felt like the decision was between continuing to work "jobs" that allowed me to make "money", or to do something different which might not be as lucrative but would lead to a bigger impact.

I decided to take the hard road, to play the long game, and do something that still might not end up working out. But instead of sitting there at a desk working a "9 to 5 job" for the rest of my life doing something I hated and wondering "what if," I chose a different path. I chose not to live with regret.

Some of this might surprise you, and some of this might not, but since you decided to pick up this book I want to share the truth with you. Admittedly, I was not the best kid growing up, let alone the best student, as you'll find out—and I certainly wasn't into learning for fun. However, somewhere around the time when I was twenty-four years old I started getting into TED Talks, which led to watching them on my lunch breaks, which led to watching select ones with my folks, which would often bring us to tears. This ultimately led to my Mom and I going to TEDxNSU (At Nova Southeastern University in Davie, Florida) four years in a row pre-Covid, where I heard some great stories from students, alumni, and professors of Nova Southeastern University in our community. This experience, which included being present for Dr. Guy Harvey's TED Talk, left a profound impression on me. My mind was expanding, learning about new people from various walks of life, as I was gaining insights unlike any I had ever obtained before. **It was this love of TED Talks, along with my friend and mentor Juan urging me to go to a monthly breakfast lecture series we'll call "CM," that ultimately led me to connect with my future business partner, Andrew Martineau, at a TEDx Simulcast event.** I was just transitioning out of recruiting at that time to "entrepreneurville" and had no idea where the road in front of me would take me—but I was wide-eyed, motivated, and hopeful.

This was around the time of the rise of Gary Vaynerchuck, aka Gary Vee, in the age of an "entrepreneurial awakening" around

2014-2016, when it felt like more and more people than ever before were leaving their jobs to pursue their passions. While still sitting at a desk recruiting I somehow stumbled across Gary on YouTube as he was blowing up in notoriety, and all it took for me was his "Six Minutes For The Next 60 Years Of Your Life" video to convince me entrepreneurship was a viable option. Gary never made it sound easy, preaching hard work and patience, but continually reminded people absorbing his content that if you're as young as I was at the time, you can "put your head down and grind for three years and if it doesn't work out you'll still be thirty-three." This encouragement inspired me to do life my way, doing the things I wanted to do—even if that was the hard way and road less traveled.

Around this time I was continually falling deeper and deeper in love with exploring the art scene, events, and taking in experiences. Somehow the universe conspired to help me become extremely passionate about pursuing my passions, at just the right moment in life when I had the ability and energy to do so. This naturally unfolded from a love of House Music (a form of electronic dance music), which I had developed slightly before venturing into the arts, courtesy of a friend inviting me to some of the incredible house music events taking place around this time in Miami where all of the leading artists in the industry would frequently play. It was at these house music events I attended, oftentimes being underground experiences in "off the beaten path locations" (for example, potentially sketchy warehouses), where I fell in love with the *"culture"* in **arts and culture**. I always loved people-watching, and these experiences brought out the best outfits for people watching. I gained a huge appreciation for the user experience of these events before I ever knew what UX (user experience) in the real world was—learning about set design, the curation of artwork at the events, the sound systems, etc. These events were being executed at the highest level with world class production teams using the very best equipment, and made for scenery you might not even find in a fairytale movie. I wish I could describe to you in words the thoughts, feelings, and emotions that resonated upon entering one of these well curated experiences I would almost anxiously await as a mere ticket holder - but you really had to be there, so for now this description will have to do. As a result of these eye opening experiences, I wanted to recreate the vibes from the "cool kid house music scene" I was experiencing in Miami, but in Fort Lauderdale which at the time was a place that wasn't regularly offering much culture aside from sporadic special events. This place I called home, I would come to find out, was often referred to as a "Cultural Wasteland"—a term which, much to my disappointment, people still use to this day. I had no idea what that meant, why high-ranking government employees would mention it in conversations, or why that term irked me to the point that I decided to do something to change it.

Fast forward, all of this led to a series of many events, with many **HIGHS AND LOWS**, and some of the toughest learning lessons of my life. These lessons left me wondering "why" more times than I care to remember, but as I progressed through them, I learned to trust in the process. Now more than ever, I am confident that these learning lessons will pay off more than they hurt at the time.

Despite my best intentions, despite being an overall "nice guy," and despite positive reinforcement from my friends and family, I just couldn't figure out why. Why didn't it work out with one thing or another, be it a girl, or a job/project, etc. I truly feel now, as I write this book, that it all ended up not working out for a reason—for me to learn, grow, and develop into the person I was destined to become. Even if it hasn't worked out the way I would have liked it to (yet), even if I had to do a lot of soul searching along the way, this is my story which I am proud to share with you. As the tagline suggests, I hope these stories and subsequent learning lessons can help you and your life, your kid's life, or the life of some kid whom you mentor and care about. Because like my friend QuickThePoet says, "We all are just a kid from somewhere," and we're all trying to find our way in this crazy world we live in, doing the best with what we've got. This is my story, and I am excited to share it with you. Thank you for trusting me with your time and attention, I promise you this will be unlike any other book you've read before.

Small note to keep in mind, I opted to write this in my own "voice" and tone. I did work with a coach, I did hire an editor as well as a formatter, and I know at times my writing and grammar might seem to be all over the place. But this was all done very intentionally to maintain my authenticity and integrity.

CHAPTER 1

Childhood (I Was The Bad Kid In School)

"It's not where you start, it's where you finish." – **Unknown**

I can't say that I started with nothing. I was fortunate enough to be born in the mid '80s to loving parents who have great hearts and great souls. My father, Michael Snow, was one of four children who grew up in New Hyde Park, Long Island, and went to North Country Community College in Saranac Lake, New York for college. My Mother, Dale Wolfe Snow, was one of three children who grew up in Allentown, Pennsylvania and graduated from Syracuse University, coincidentally also in upstate New York. My father came from a hard-working blue collar family; my grandfather was a plumber in the Bronx, and I understand they got by with very modest means. My mother came from more of a white collar family. Her father was an optometrist and successful businessman, after her grandfather had been an even more successful businessman and the owner of Phoenix Clothes, which eventually sold to Genesco.

Fortunately for me, they both decided they never wanted to deal with lake-effect snow again, so the universe brought them down to South Florida, for which I'm forever grateful. The way the story goes, or at least the way I'll tell it, somehow they met, without a cell phone or the internet in the 1970s. That "somehow" had to do with Werner Erhard's EST Training personal development seminars, the early pre-stages of what's now known as *Landmark Education* (aka The Landmark Forum). These EST training seminars aimed to "transform one's ability to experience living so that the situations one had been trying to change or had been putting up with clear up just in the process of life itself." Needless to say, I was born with the DNA of parents who care about their own development and the growth of those around them.

My parents progressed through Werner Erhard's Landmark series of seminars to the advanced course and beyond, eventually leading and facilitating at the early stages of this organization whose work predates what would be more commonly associated with Gratitude Training. This impact of their kindness, generosity, and patience with me as a child undoubtedly had a positive impact on my life, which I want to provide context for and highlight. They brought me to seminars from an early age and had me attend *The Forum For Young People* when I was in fifth grade, where I learned about "not running a racket" (in your mind) of negative thoughts.

As they were preparing to have me in the mid '80s, my parents made a choice to buy a new home in a little western Broward

County suburb called Coral Springs, which still had strawberry fields and horses around it. Coral Springs is a beautiful suburban community bordering the Everglades, lined with trees, great landscaping, and over one hundred parks with tons of things for kids to do in a great place to raise a family. I played sports, did karate, tumbled, went to Hebrew school and temple until I was bar-mitzvahed, had play dates, and overall, enjoyed a great childhood. Until I started approaching my teenage years, when unfortunately I learned to choose some bad habits that led to an unintentional negative effect on my development in school.

Despite being around smart kids, being involved with student government (although I was never elected), and playing lacrosse/basketball in sports organizations, the traditional school system did not resonate with me. It wasn't until I was much older, listening to the likes of Gary Vee and Joe Rogan that I understood I was not alone in this situation.

A lot of people try to explain things in life by saying, "The book says…" Well, the book says you should do a lot of things, but what book is this? Don't they make new versions of these books? And update them as needed? Well, *this* book is going to tell you something different, as this is not a self-help book. I am going to keep it 100% real with you and let you know that in life, not everything is peaches and roses.

As I was growing up and entering middle school, I tended to **subconsciously** do the opposite of what the book said to do. Most notably, as far back as I can remember to fourth grade, my friends and classmates would urge me to speak out in class and say the things everyone was thinking that no one wanted to say, because it would earn them a trip to internal or even external suspension. I can remember starting to get in real trouble while in elementary school around the fourth grade with a teacher whom my mother recounts as being terrible, but it wasn't as much of a warning sign at the time like it would be today. I do remember eventually getting sent to the principal's office in elementary school at a much earlier age than I should have, and realizing to myself "I probably shouldn't be here, I don't belong here." But the mind is so fragile at that age, how are you supposed to decipher what is going on when you're just going through the motions of school, lunchtime, P.E., rinse and repeat. By the time fifth grade rolled around I had a great teacher (Mrs. Ramu-Adler) whom I adored. Yet despite this admiration, I found myself getting in enough trouble that I was the only kid not allowed to go on the fifth grade school trip to Washington, D.C. My little brain wasn't able to process at the time that missing out on these opportunities and others would ultimately set me back further and further into a hole that inevitably took me 20+ years to overcome.

By the time I got into middle school the ante was up, and with new kids and new pressures I was rising to a challenge I shouldn't have tried to meet. Also, while my elementary school was a relatively safe place actually located in my residential neighborhood, Forest Glen Middle School was a little more ethnically diverse. There were more kids from various backgrounds and Caribbean cultures including Cubans, Puerto Ricans, Haitians, Colombians, Jamaicans, Dominicans, etc.

I somehow found myself spending quite a bit of time in the suspension and detention halls, with approximately 50% of the school days during my seventh grade year being spent in internal suspension. While I was hurting a lot in the process of trying to find out more about myself the hard way, I was also learning a lot about myself and life. Forest Glen Middle School, while in middle-class suburban Coral Springs, at one point was reported as having a 90% African American student body with a large majority of those kids being bussed in from the neighboring city of Pompano, which at the time had many lower income housing projects and not enough desks for all of the students within their city limits. Fortunately throughout this experience I was also surrounded by many people from South America and the Caribbean Islands, developing friendships with Colombians, Haitians, Puerto Ricans, and many other nationalities in between. I credit these diverse experiences at a young age with helping me to not look at people of color or immigration status the same way many other white kids from the suburbs did. This inevitably led the way to partnering with a Trinidadian native who immigrated to this country in pursuit of his American Dream, teaching me more about race than any school book could at the height of our modern day race relations.

Around this middle school period of my life, I had started playing lacrosse with the Coral Springs Tomahawks youth lacrosse club before the game blew up in popularity and became an in- school sport. I guess because it wasn't in the school system as a sanctioned sport (it was club at that time), and that my parents didn't exactly threaten me with taking the game away from me despite my indiscretions, lacrosse became a safe space for me to escape and be with the boys after long days of school. I look back at an alternative school called Cross Creek that the counselors mentioned (don't think they ever really threatened) to sending me to, along with military boarding schools, and think to myself if I didn't have sports (I also enjoyed playing basketball in middle school), that I could have gone down a much darker path. I do want to credit my parents for their patience, love, and bringing me to leading local child psychologists, which ultimately did help me progress to being a functioning member of society.

Not every kid I grew up with was so fortunate to find these experiences, the bad and the good ones. While I was growing up in the relatively safe confines of Coral Springs, I unfortunately knew more kids who passed away before I turned eighteen than I have in my last eighteen years between car accidents and oxycontin overdoses. When I say I'm working hard now to make my parents proud, it's to make up for the years of disappointment I left them with as a child. Thankfully their loving guidance kept me from delving down different paths I could have fallen victim to that wouldn't have allowed me this opportunity to make them proud today. Though it wasn't easy, as I can't tell you how many times they must have heard, "Evan has all the potential in the world" from the assistant principals while picking me up from school after an incident. I still vividly remember hearing them saying to my parents "He just can't figure it out" – but as we discovered later in life, the school system wasn't for me. Though, a lot of things weren't for me. Maybe Coral Springs wasn't for me, maybe Boy Scouts wasn't for me, maybe being an '80s baby wasn't for me, maybe I was born ahead of my time. But this was the hand I was dealt, and it's not about the hand you're dealt in life—it's about how you play your cards.

There were a lot of things that weren't for me. The kids I grew up with who didn't end up being my lifelong friends weren't for me. I was different, I was an outlier, and I was destined for something bigger—something greater. Over twenty years later, as I found my voice becoming an arts advocate and a community builder, I discovered passions I never knew existed. As I learned when my throat chakra opened, those experiences truly did pave the way for my voice to be heard in more impactful ways than "what the book said" or ever could say back then. The book unfortunately did not say to try and support the arts in a place where people really didn't care about the visual arts to the extent they should have (Fort Lauderdale/Broward County). The book would not have said do all of these things altruistically at your own expense and time when in all actuality there might never be a payback or a return on investment. That's why I am writing **this book**, to hopefully touch and inspire one life: your life, your kid's life, or that kid's life you want to impact because you know they are destined for greatness. I am thirty-seven years old now and I always knew I was capable and destined for something more. I never knew how great or what greatness would become, but here are a few things we've accomplished in the first seven years of my art/community building career beyond what I ever could have imagined in my wildest dreams:

- Co-founded 4 companies and 2 non-profits from the ground up with no outside funding, all starting with a hashtag. #Choose954

- Helped put 105 artificial reefs into the ocean off the coast of southeast Florida—80 in Palm Beach and 25 in Hollywood in my native home county of Broward (while still not a diver or marine biologist). This led to new patents, augmentations, and innovations being created in the coral outplanting sector of marine biology, and might inevitably contribute to a solution in the race to save our world's coral reefs by keeping the momentum going and connecting some much needed dots.

- Produced 4 annual art fairs and 5 county wide art weeks without major sponsorship, exhibiting over 500 artists and 1000+ pieces of artwork inside mansions our attendees could only access via boat—changing artist lives multiple times over just through Art Fort Lauderdale alone.

- Hosted 155 consecutive weeks of live art pop-ups, the "Choose954 Local Artist Discovery Series" pre-Covid at YOLO on Las Olas Boulevard, giving multiple artists their first opportunity to ever exhibit in public and changing countless lives multiple times over. I still hear success stories years later I could never have imagined (and hope you guys will share more with me I wasn't aware of).

- Hosted years of monthly breakfast lectures, speaker series, fireside chats, and panel discussions with now over 100 speakers—bringing insight, connection, and inspiration to our community all for free as it was provided for me one January morning in 2016.

- Opened 28 affordable artist studio locations in 3 states (and counting), 7 counties, with over 400 artists coming through the program in the first 4 years, leading to countless collaborations, commissions, and success stories for ourselves/artists/property owners alike.

- Hosted over 150 podcasts between 3 different series (Choose954, Zero Empty Spaces, Art Fort Lauderdale) telling many local legends' stories that might not have been shared otherwise

- Helped start a chapter of Axen Club, a goal-setting/accountability group (mini mastermind) that helped inspire and change multiple lives in our community countless times over—most notably our friend Enid who started RAW Story Telling (our version of "The Moth") which led to her branding agency RAW Made.

CHAPTER 2

The 7 Moments That Changed My Life

"Life is like a game of cards, you play the hand you're dealt, and can't win by folding. Sometimes you have to take a chance if you want to win." - **Ellsworth "Bumpy" Johnson, as portrayed by Forest Whitaker in "The Godfather of Harlem" TV series.**

They say life is full of choices, and this book is a small testament to that and how these distinct moments influenced the course of my life and can hopefully help you influence yours. After *grooving through life* for my first thirty years as a "regular guy," I decided to move to Downtown Fort Lauderdale, Florida with two friends I enjoyed hanging out with, where my life would soon undoubtedly change for the better. Coming from the suburbs of Coral Springs in western Broward County, I had no idea what living in an urban environment and thrusting myself into the community would do for me. This happened at a very serendipitous time in my life and in the world, as there was an **entrepreneurial shift** going on with more and more people leaving their *jobs* to pursue their **passions** or side hustles than ever before, and I would soon become one of them.

I would like to thank the likes of some very inspirational/ motivational people whose content I was pumping in my ears at that time while I was still a recruiter working a desk job in the corporate world. Most notably Simon Sinek, who preached to "Start With Why" (one of the most watched TED Talks of all time), and Gary Vaynerchuk aka "Gary Vee" – who I fell in love with at the time. At that time Gary was becoming one of the foremost thought leaders on preaching others to pursue entrepreneurship, not to do shit you hated, and that "1 > 0". I'll never forget the first time I listened to his YouTube video titled "6 minutes for the next 60 years of your life," where he simply reminded myself and his audience that "you can put your head down and grind for three years, and if it doesn't work out you're still thirty-three years old." Upon diving deeper into Gary Vee, TED Talks, and other forms of inspiration at that time which all felt so new to me, I was slowly becoming empowered to take control of my life. It was a culmination of this inspiration/ empowerment, mixed with the impact of the following seven moments that changed my life, which led me down the path I've pursued for the last 7+ years and plan to continue for the next sixty.

I can vividly remember these seven key moments, making subtle choices that didn't seem like much at the time, but would be catalysts for major changes and shifts in my life. While there were many moments along the way that stick out, and while I might say "this has had a profound impact on my life" more than others, these are the *choices I made* and moments that really did;

- Going to Wynwood during Miami Art Week the first time in 2014
- Moving to Downtown Fort Lauderdale in 2015
- First time taking psilocybin (magic mushrooms) and discovering Boiler Room in 2015
- Attending a monthly breakfast lecture series in January 2016 - My "Aha moment"
- Meeting my future business partner Andrew in 2016
- Discovering and developing my yoga practice in 2020
- Discovering men's work and joining a conscious men's group in 2022

Of course there were other moments before, after, and in between. I learned valuable lessons growing up playing lacrosse with my father as one of my coaches who preached hard work, to play the game with integrity, and to live your life with character which he framed as doing good even when no one else was watching. I was fortunate enough to have friends and mentors come into my life who saw things inside of me that I didn't see in myself at the time (thankfully a recurring theme), and who were kind enough to take the time out of their lives to work with me to develop myself to my truest potential. There were countless talks, workshops, and expos I attended where I was fortunate enough to hear brilliant minds share their stories and insights, which undoubtedly left their mark on me. During most of these moments, I could never have imagined the impact they'd be having on my life at the time. In writing this book I could think of dozens of moments to recount, but for now we're going to dive deeper into these seven, look at the learning lessons that follow, and see how the takeaways can apply to create breakthroughs in your life.

CHAPTER 3

Learning To Choose: Art, Culture, And House Music

"It's not who you are that holds you back, it's who you think you're not" - **Jean-Michel Basquiat**

Sometime around 2013-2014, there was a major cultural revolution in South Florida and beyond, slightly before there was an entrepreneurial revolution in 2015 we'll dive into later. Around this time the prevalence of street art, more specifically murals, was becoming more and more commonplace on the walls in cities across the country and globe. Nowhere, and I literally mean NOWHERE was this more prevalent than the midtown, industrial, warehouse section of Miami adjacent to Overtown, in what is now called "Wynwood." An area where, just a few years before this you wouldn't stop your car if you had a flat tire, was quickly becoming the place you stopped your car to take photos of incredible displays of public art on the walls of rundown warehouses.

It was explained to me through second hand knowledge from street art historians/curators that Tony Goldman, the uber successful developer behind the SoHo redevelopment and revolution, turned to his kids one day and said, "We have all the money we need to do anything we want to do, what do you want to do now?" and it was his son (not daughter who now runs Goldman Global Properties and Goldman Arts) who said, "I want to make the largest public outdoor art museum." If you've never been there, Wynwood became just that, a place where everywhere you looked—every wall (and a lot of the sidewalk) had murals, not just by talented local artists but by the best of the best in the world to ever hold a spray can.

Even though in 2014 I was not into art per se, there was enough buzz and murmurs through things like Foursquare and Myspace that I was called to go to Wynwood for the first time (for art), by myself, during this thing called "Art Basel" (the leading art fair in the world). The only way I can describe pulling up to the corner of Twenty-Fifth Street and North Miami Avenue was that it was like a movie, or maybe more like a movie set without the cameras. There were sprawling murals, neon light installations, shipping containers converted into art gallery experiences, with true modern contemporary paintings, and photographs on metallic prints which absolutely had me enthralled.

Remember the first time you went to Disney World? Harry Potter Land? Meow Wolf? Yes! It's that first impression, that awestruck, blown away, "whoa" factor—this indeed was my vibe way before I had met my tribe. Little did I know this was just the outskirts, but little did it matter to me as you can see in those first photos I took with my camera phone that are still in my Facebook albums. That first trip to Wynwood, I think I only ventured one or two blocks over the course of three hours, but that was all I needed to see. I spent my evening exploring the glass blowers, the photographers, the muralists, and the people there to see and be seen who made up this scene. Imagine walking on to a movie set in Hollywood for the first time and being transported into another world with characters unlike any movie you've seen before—this was what I was experiencing, and I loved it.

It was after that first breathtaking art experience that I developed a yearning for more, and subsequently did not pass up an opportunity to go to Wynwood over the next few years whenever anyone would ask or whenever there was a relevant event on the calendar. Be it for an entrepreneurial lecture series with the likes of Zak The Baker sharing his story, or an arts+culture experience like the Secret Garden (one of my favorites), or pop-up underground house music events with some of the best DJs in the world visiting Miami—I was there. Little did I know but would soon find out that I was collecting so much in terms of knowledge, connections, and memories from these enriching experiences as a mere patron, I was slowly becoming a changed person. I quickly became a part of the scene, a member of the community, and I fell in love with it.

But before this first art experience, came my first taste of "culture" on my first trip to Wynwood. I will never forget, and am forever eternally grateful for, a dear friend of mine who later became my roommate, who we'll call "Lefty". Lefty was a professional poker player from Memphis by way of Honduras who truly lived the Pura Vida life, indulging in all of the things his heart desired. I highly admired and respected David as a world class poker player, and had heard from mutual friends the legendary stories of his nightlife adventures, which sounded appealing to me in my late twenties. More so than a party-loving World Series of Poker Championship professional gambler, David was actually a music aficionado who was working on his own personal development journey through reading various books and listening to podcasts, which didn't resonate with me until much later but have indelibly left their mark (wish I would've started listening to Joe Rogan with him sooner, but it is what it is now). After we connected through co-workers and mutual friends from Memphis and became fast friends, Lefty shared an invitation with me that I can truly say changed the course of my life, with a few words I'll never forget.

"We're going to see this guy at a show (an "underground" music festival) in Wynwood." The year was 2014, the music festival was III Points in its second year, and the guy was none other than Australian singer Chet Faker.

Not only do I think it will never be the same, I don't think there will ever be another place like this place was at that time. I'm sure I missed some of the glory days, but thankfully I was present while things were still on the way up to the peak before the commercialization and "Wynwood Effect" took over, when the prices of commercial real estate rose to the point the true artists could not afford to be there anymore and condos were built on the sites where these warehouses that served as art studios used to stand. Nevertheless, thinking back on that first III Points experience at MAPS Backlot… Man. The vibe, the people, the music, while all still new and fresh to my eyes, ears, and soul, touched me in a way nothing has ever touched me before. After that first experience, I developed an indelible zest for more. It was unlike anything I'd ever experienced before and might not ever experience again, aside from diving deeper into my yoga journey (but different). It was all so new to me, so rich, so vibrant, and so enriching. Looking back at it I can't help but think, "Man, am I glad I did that," as I learned how to step outside of my comfort zone to the unknown.

It was like a learning of how to learn, or what I later learned as "un-learning" that was reshaping my mind in a positive, expansive manner. This is where I was meant to be, this is what I was meant to see, and this is what I was meant to develop into on this crazy journey called life. This learning, coupled with the fact that these events and experiences took place just 30-45 minutes to the south of me in Miami, paved the way for the future version of myself to want to develop similar experiences in my community. I didn't really know what community building was at the time, let alone creative entrepreneurship, or even placemaking – but I would soon find out and develop into all three of those categories as naturally as possible. The flame was lit inside of me, and despite an uphill road ahead to try and replicate these experiences in my community, nothing would put that flame out.

Discovering "Bedside"

Simultaneously around this time I was developing a knack for discovering new music in these expansive genres on a platform that was foreign to me called *Soundcloud*. Soundcloud is a place where musicians, DJs, and producers of any level can upload their music to be discovered and played by the masses. This was considered the "golden age of the Soundcloud Era" I came to find out later from the likes of DJ Joe Kay (founder of Soulection

Radio), and that discovering hidden talent on this platform was the modern version of "digging in the crates" similar to what music lovers used to have to do back in the day with vinyl records. Well, while I was "digging" virtually and exploring new genres, I stumbled across an upcoming event in the Little Haiti neighborhood of Miami with a featured "horn driven DJ/producer duo" that piqued my interest. I began listening to their original tracks and mixes on Soundcloud and was instantly drawn into a new, unique sound that I would describe as a hybrid between "tropical melodical house music" mixed with new age and futuristic sounds with live instruments sprinkled on top. In my opinion the music was then, and is still now, ahead of its time, but this duo I came to learn of as "Bedside" was having a moment in the Miami Music Scene.

At this first live event I attended, I was met with even more compelling cool vibes than I had previously seen in Wynwood. The venue in the Little Haiti area of Miami was called "The Citadel" which had become a rundown warehouse of sorts slated to be redeveloped into a food hall in an area I had no idea would inevitably become gentrified. I came to find that these spaces (similar to Wynwood) were part of the recipe for really cool "underground events" as most people would consider them. Sponsored by Beck's beer and produced by an emerging cultural curator who had recently launched her "Defy Culture Agency" at that time, this event on June 23, 2016, called "Becks Urban Canvas" shined a light on five emerging visual artists each with their own unique style. These artists were provided a large canvas in the form of pop-up walls they were able to "muralize" with spray paint during the event, including one collaborative wall where they all put their own spin on the Beck's logo. It was the smell of the fresh spray paint, mixed with the tastes of bites courtesy of Chef Creole who was blowing up at that time, mixed with the awe inspiring people-watching I came to find at these events that really blew my mind.

Throughout the night I was recognizing people I had begun following on social media who were serving as inspiration for me, most notably a woman by the name of "Izzy" who was running an organization called "Prism Creative Group" at the time. Prism was doing an amazing job of curating and storytelling the cultural experiences I was seeking then, with tasteful aesthetics, well delivered messaging, and phenomenal photos that would give anyone FOMO. I introduced myself to Izzy, who met my kind words and positive feedback on her efforts with a warm reception, which I remember being very comforting at that time. Among other people I met that night, there was a mutual friend of Izzy's and the events curator who went by the name of "Rosy", who within the first thirty seconds of meeting me somehow read my mind and knew the mission I was on in life as I was still figuring it out. That chance interaction, and her accurate reading of my mind with no prior knowledge of who I was, was still one of the most mind blowing interactions I ever had with a random stranger who inevitably became a friend and supporter. As the night progressed, I was really feeling great and having a fabulous time with my culture-loving friend and mentor Juan and his cousin who was also a DJ by the name of Los. We were vibing, taking photos, seeing the sights, and taking it all in. And then the headliners **Bedside** began taking the stage.

I had recently connected with Bedside on social media, letting their manager who ran the page know I was quickly becoming a big fan and was excited to attend this event after extensively playing their musical collection on Soundcloud. About halfway through the event, as the warm-up DJ was wrapping up and Bedside was taking the stage, I was met by a kind woman on the dance floor area in front of where the music was being played who handed me a sticker I quickly recognized as their logo from their pages. The woman introduced herself as Lauren, otherwise known as "LP", and she thanked me for being supportive of the group that was comprised of her fiancé Travis Acker and Trace Barfield. We chatted some, vibed out, danced, and had a grand ol' time as Bedside played this live performance with a five-piece band including a saxophone player, percussion keyboardist,

Travis on the bass, and Trace with the EWI (electronic wind instrument) in addition to his signature trumpet. I quickly fell in love with this unique sound, and before I knew it, I would become Bedside's biggest fan, making it to nearly every one of their many live shows as they were being scheduled almost monthly throughout Miami. I came to find out that this was in part due to the fact that LP was deeply connected into the local music scene as a fellow writer/blogger with her own "South Florida Music Obsessed" blog (aka SFMO), in addition to being the Public Relations Director for the III Points music festival I had recently discovered. It was all serendipitously coming together in ways I could never have forecasted, before I even knew what serendipity was.

While I was continually playing their ever evolving series of "Horizon Mix" masterpieces on Soundcloud, reposting to my friends and followers in my early culture blogging days, LP took notice. She saw something in me that maybe I didn't see in myself yet, and befriended me, building a relationship around our shared passions of art, culture, travel, and of course her beloved Bedside group. It was at this time that I was being more and more called to recreate these Miami experiences in Fort Lauderdale, especially with the house music scene I had now fallen in love with. When I reached out to LP with no venue, no real experience or money, and really without a clue of what I was doing, asking if we could book Bedside in Fort Lauderdale, she didn't shoot me down like 99% of everyone else I reached out to in Miami did. She was kind enough to take the time in guiding and mentoring me along my transition from recruiter to food blogger to community builder and event producer, while continually checking to see how I was doing and how she could help. This was all while serving as PR Director for the ever evolving III Points festival that was continually rising in prominence and notoriety that provided tremendous inspiration for my fascination with festivals and experiences. While most of the Bedside events were free and open at some really cool venues throughout Miami at the time like Bardot and The SLS, LP invited me to the members only "SoHo Beach House" in Miami Beach for one of their few private events as a guest of hers. It was these invitations, shared experiences, conversations, and ultimately her and Bedside's acceptance of me as a fan and friend that meant the most to me. I felt seen, and I felt there was a mutual reciprocation of appreciation for each other's support—my support for Bedside's music and Bedside's support of me as their loyal #1 fan. When Lauren couldn't attend events she would ask me to shoot pictures and videos for social media, which I was glad and honored to do. I had a feeling Bedside was on the way to stardom with their sound being just ahead of its time, and that I might even get to go along for the ride if and when they began traveling and touring.

As I transitioned into entrepreneurship and shortly thereafter launched Art Fort Lauderdale "The Art Fair On The Water" with my newfound business partner Andrew, Lauren helped me achieve my goal of having Bedside play in Fort Lauderdale at our inaugural VIP Opening Vernissage Reception. She even helped us get our first monetary sponsor for the fair the next year through a personal connection she had to Hoffman's Chocolates, who provided us with unique chocolate popups at the fair and our opening party. Things were looking up, and I thought this upwards trajectory would carry me to the promised land and beyond.

Unfortunately, the universe sometimes works in mysterious ways, and I came to find out the reason LP couldn't always attend the events was because she was battling leukemia and lymphoma. While she was able to stay in positive spirits through our conversations, unfortunately the debilitating disease was taking its toll on her, and LP passed away on September 17, 2018 at the early age of thirty-six. As I reflect on this time of my life, the feeling of being welcomed and accepted by Lauren and this group that I fell in love with when they didn't have to created a feeling inside of me at a time in my life when I was going through uncertain transitions that undoubtedly had a life changing effect on me.

While understandably Bedside as a group did not continue, their music lives forever in my heart and in my headphones. Their timeless music has been one of the most comforting resources I can turn to, especially during my plant medicine journeys (which I'll expand on later), and has helped remind me of many great memories along the way up until writing today. It was a few years ago on one of these **plant medicine journeys** when I received a *"message"* that I really didn't know how to translate into words, but have since had years to reflect upon and better decipher. The message, delivered non verbally and almost energetically (the best way I can explain it) essentially translated to "don't let them forget about me." After much thought, deliberation, further journeying, and conversation with friends and confidants, I felt called to launch the "My Sweetest LP" arts writing scholarship in honor of Lauren to give a student at her University of Florida alma mater a boost on their journey towards pursuing their passion of covering the arts similar to how we had done. I was fortunate enough that one of the confidants I shared this idea with over lunch was one of my Zero Empty Spaces resident artists (Bob Peckar) who had the talent, ability, and generosity to take our conversation along with some of my creative vision and create a beautiful piece of artwork he decided to donate as part of a silent auction for this cause, with the proceeds kicking off this arts writing scholarship. The hope and goal is that the recipient of this arts writing scholarship will be able to cover the arts and culture while in college or after graduating, receive writing opportunities from the platforms I'm involved with among other friends' organizations, and that they can provide much needed editorial coverage of the arts in a time when arts writing unfortunately is not as valued as it once was. And I hope that maybe one day the recipient of this grant receives the inspiration, support, and opportunity to contribute to changing the world the way LP and I did. #RIPLP

Learning lesson

I want you to take a moment to think about this: What is your favorite passion or hobby? What is your second favorite? How did you discover that? Did it happen immediately? Or was it nurtured over time? Maybe falling in love with art, or house music, or community building isn't the passion for you, but I'm hoping reading these versions of my story can help trigger something for you. Maybe to discover new passions or hobbies? Or maybe rediscover old ones? You never know where they might lead and how they might change your life, or the lives of those in your community.

Chapter 4

Learning To Choose The "Aha Moment"

"The price of greatness is responsibility" - **Sir Winston Churchill**

After living the majority of my life in the quiet western suburbs of Broward County (Coral Springs, Coconut Creek, Boca Raton area), in 2015 I was ready to venture out east and move to downtown Fort Lauderdale. Previously, some of my living experiences came to unfortunate ends, with places I rented getting broken into and couples I shared houses with separating prematurely. But this time, I reached a mutual agreement with two brothers from Honduras by way of Memphis who had become good social friends of mine, and we got an apartment in the Camden Building. One of these brothers ("Lefty") was the one I mentioned earlier who initially took me to my first house music experience with III Points in Wynwood prior to us moving in together. I had admired Lefty for years as a successful professional poker player and legend amongst men for some of his late-night partying stories. Having survived a childhood bout with bone cancer that claimed one of his arms but left him with a new outlook on life thanks to the good folks at St. Jude Children's Hospital, Lefty operated differently than any of the poker players I knew in my previous life as a semiprofessional/recreational poker player. While our initial social outings began with going out to sports bars to watch the Miami Heat and football games, followed by exploring chef-inspired *craft food* restaurants, it was ultimately the love of music—in particular, the house music to which Lefty introduced me—that truly opened my eyes to worlds I didn't know existed.

This new chapter in my life all fortunately happened around the time I was discovering III Points, house music, and the Miami Art Scene in 2014-2015, which would pave the way for me to develop a budding desire to recreate the magic I had begun experiencing down the road in Miami with my 954 community. Shortly before moving in late 2014, I met a young woman at a training seminar who began telling me on break she would make a couple of bucks by writing a **blog** about the free items provided to her by a company at the time (Thank You Molly!). The items, such as watches, shoes, and gadgets, were pretty cool and in line with modern culture, which I could attribute to being kind of "Robb Robert-esque," and while I wasn't compelled to write a blog for those exact same reasons, a seed was planted in my brain. It's crazy to think back just a few short years ago before *influencer marketing* was a thing, back in the days of Foursquare and early days of Instagram, local businesses would really value and appreciate you supporting them by posting about their venue online. I always had a love for food and restaurants, and with an upcoming plan of moving to a downtown place like Fort Lauderdale with more chef-inspired restaurants closely available to me than in the suburbs, I was slowly considering starting a food blog. Around the time Yelp was becoming popular in 2014, I was formulating a skill of discovering really cool hidden-gem restaurants and posting pictures/checkins on Foursquare and Facebook, but I wasn't *really doing anything with them at the time*. My friends would always say they "liked the places 'Snow' stopped at" (since I go by my last name amongst friends). After the introduction and some encouragement to begin a blog, I subsequently named it "Snows Stops Food Blog" to show my friends and family all of the places "Snow Stopped At", which they generally liked and appreciated. I was quickly being associated as a "foodie" and had no idea where this journey would inevitably take me, but I was down for the adventure.

Initially, I posted only two blogs in late 2014 while I was still working in the recruiting world, and had no idea how this blogging thing could change my life. It wasn't until I attended an event one morning in 2016 when it all "clicked" for me, which to this day, I attribute as my **"aha moment."** My friend and mentor Juan had been working out of a co-working space in downtown Fort Lauderdale not far from me, and he too was a fan of motivational/inspirational talks similar to TED talks. At this time the co-working space was hosting something new to me: a monthly breakfast lecture series referred to as a "mini TED Talk" held for free. I came to find out this was part of a bigger global community with chapters in 180 cities at the time, which helped spark a lightbulb in my mind about being part of something larger than just my own community. Although the first few talks I attended were not overwhelmingly inspirational to me, the one which did it for me was on that one fateful morning in January 2016, with a speaker I had recently begun following who would be talking on the topic of *language*. The speaker, Alexa Rose Carlin, shared her own thought-provoking and inspiring story. She had been an aspiring college student pursuing a career in the fashion industry in NYC, seemingly having much success on a clear path early on in her journey to success. Then, however, she developed sepsis and needed to be placed in a coma. She shared how she had a 1% chance of living and how she had seen herself running through a field of green grass like an out of body experience while in the coma, hooked up to dozens of machines. Fortunately, she was able to get through it and return to living a normal, functional life with a new purpose. In sharing how she learned and grew from that experience to become an author, speaker, and eventually the founder of a popular women's empowerment conference called Women Empower X (WEX), her words resonated with me in a way that almost seemed like destiny for me to be hearing them at that time. I was truly dialed in, and had no idea that this would be the morning that would change my life, my community, and inevitably even the art world.

She wasn't speaking about the *languages* of English, Hebrew, or Spanish. She was sharing more on how "if you speak the language of positivity you will portray positivity, and if you speak the language of unworthiness your actions will portray negatively." But more so than that, she was encouraging the audience to "be genuine, be authentic, and pursue your passions." It had been a few years since I had pursued a passion in attempting to play poker semi-professionally with mixed success, and there was a fire that was being lit inside of me as that lightbulb went off. She also suggested that the attendees of this talk should record a video on their phones after leaving about what they planned to do with this new found inspiration, and I felt called to seriously further pursue this idea I had been kicking around for having a food blog. There wasn't really a handbook, or many influential food bloggers at that time showing or telling how they were monetizing their efforts, so the idea didn't exactly jump off the table at first. But the thought of doing something I wanted to do and loved doing (and potentially getting free meals out of it) sounded appealing at a time when I was making a modest living as a recruiter.

Well, the way the story goes is, food blogging got my name and social media pages out there, which got me invited to events like tastings, pairings, openings, festivals, etc. Going to events earned me the opportunity to meet the marketing and public relations people coordinating these events, and meeting these folks made me realize—I can do these events too! With this new found motivation, fueled by more inspiration from Gary Vee and others, I began exploring more, diving deeper down the culinary rabbit holes in South Florida. I was doing my part not only in discovering *hidden-gem restaurants* few people in the community knew about, but highlighting them through my own creative lens and voice. I always had an affinity for local independent businesses over big corporate chains, be it the local barbershop over a nationwide salon, or the family owned local restaurant over a franchise you see in every city. I was beginning to witness how these local small businesses were the backbones of communities as the "Support Local" movement was rising, and I wanted to further show and tell this story to my friends, family, and followers. It was becoming clear to me that the places I enjoyed visiting on my travels in cities like Austin, Nashville, and Asheville were a large part of what made the communities they were a part of great - and I wanted this for my native Broward County. I just needed a larger vehicle, or platform to be able to do so than just a **food blog**.

Choose954 Story

It was my love of food and exploring new restaurants, cultures, and experiences that ultimately led us to where we are today with you reading this story. Around this time of moving to downtown Fort Lauderdale and diving deeper into food blogging and exploring the arts, I was feeling more and more called to share these experiences I was discovering with a wider audience than just my friends and family. Initially, this started with my own food blog, followed by posting more on social media, followed by various dinner invitations. But there were more and more new cool things I was discovering that I felt a calling to show my community on a grander scale. I also kept noticing that while I was going around town in East Fort Lauderdale, about thirty-five minutes from where I grew up in the suburbs of Coral Springs, I wasn't encountering any of the people I grew up with. Sure, it had been a few years since my generation (Coral Springs High School class of 2004) had left to go to college and start their adult lives, but I felt there was something missing. I felt that, especially at this time, Fort Lauderdale and Broward County were sandwiched between Miami to the south and Palm Beach to the north, oftentimes being overshadowed and forgotten as a *cultural wasteland* (not my term). Yet there was a burgeoning scene of new culture that was still somewhat "underground" or yet to be discovered, and I felt if I could just

SHOW the people I grew up with what was going on where they were originally from it would give them reasons to *"Choose The 954"* and maybe eventually come back.

My friends and roommates at the time were from Memphis, Tennessee, and they keyed me into a social movement from their hometown called "Choose901" (901 being the area code in Memphis). It would periodically come up in conversation when friends of theirs would visit from Memphis and make a comical reference that my roommate Lefty wouldn't "Choose901" anymore because he seldom came back home. Needless to say, I was intrigued and wanted to find out more about this Choose901 movement.

I started following their social media pages and seeing the messages they were putting out about community events and initiatives, and couldn't help but take a liking to it. "There are people that know and believe Memphis isn't becoming a good city, but already is a great city," the about section on their website would boast. "Choose901 exists to share these great things and introduce these great people to each other while being a positive megaphone to the rest of the world." Reading this really started to resonate with me, and this resonance, cemented with "now is the time, Memphis is the place," made me decide I needed to check this place out.

It wasn't until I decided to make the trek to Memphis for the World Championship BBQ Festival during their famed "Memphis In May" month-long celebration in 2016 when I saw the impact of this movement firsthand. I discovered from reaching out and speaking with one of the co-founders of Choose901 that they initially started as a movement by the Church to provide computer training and resources to those in the community for career advancement, and eventually evolved into a movement acquired by the City to recruit teachers, paramedics, and firefighters to live and work in Memphis. Unfortunately, while this is a city of great history and culture, Memphis has been home to two of the five worst neighborhoods in the country, and as a result, it has had its own civic struggles.

With fresh eyes I was able to see past the bad and really focus on the good, the way that these community builders had made an impact with their social movement on a place that wasn't so big on social media at the time. I really loved the way they would have local creatives put together cool t-shirts encapsulating the uniqueness of their community, and do occasional pop-ups where there would be lines around the corner until they sold out. And I was impressed by the way they could rally together for another festival that their community supported and embraced outside of Memphis In May with their 901 Day on September 1st every year. I thought to myself, this is a proven, replicable model that could benefit my community. Needless to say, I had a blast at BBQ fest thanks to my Memphis friends who showed me a VIP experience way beyond the traditional "General Admission" experience, and Memphis forever gained a special place in my heart. If you ever get an opportunity to go to the World Championship BBQ Festival, it really spans more than a mile along the Mississippi River, and really is worth adding to your bucket list.

I came back from this trip, one of my early "culture crusades" where I purely went to explore the arts and culture landscape, supercharged with a breath of fresh air. I quickly realized before I knew about the politics and drama behind the scenes that the problems in our community weren't even really "that bad"; we just needed a little more arts and culture. At this time there was a burgeoning arts district that had a monthly art walk which was starting to get a hundred or so people to come out during the last Saturday night of every month, but most of the arts initiatives across the county were still relatively scattered then. This was in May 2016, and just a few weeks after returning from Memphis, while spending some time in what's now known as the former FATVillage Arts District of Fort Lauderdale ("Flagler Village"), I had a calling to start **Choose954**. More so than just sharing about food, I wanted to highlight the arts that were having a profound impact on my view of the world at this time by "**cultivating culture and community**"—which I set out on a mission to do. The beginnings were very modest, all starting with a hashtag on a few social media posts on my own personal Facebook. Then I created the Choose954 social media pages, followed by filling up the Facebook events calendar on that page with curated local events, and launching a podcast to tell the stories of local community members doing important things, and eventually publishing a bi-weekly culture roundup newsletter that would reach 20,000+ local subscribers with whom I would share the "cool things to do." People would tell me around this time that I went to "all of the coolest events," and they didn't want to scour through ten different pages or sites to find one thing to do. So, I tried to simplify that for them and make this content easily available on Choose954's Facebook and Instagram where most of people's attention was being directed at that time.

Looking back at it now, somehow the universe serendipitously put me in place to have all of this unfold organically, so that when I would meet my soon-to-be business partner just a few short weeks afterwards (which I'll tell you about shortly), I had this "Choose954" project I was beginning to work on which was able to catch his attention. If it wasn't for food blogging, if it wasn't for my roommates being from Memphis and unintentionally telling me about Choose901, if it wasn't for getting inspired via TED Talks, this all might have been a "what-if" scenario. I hear people like Gary Vee talk about "Regret is the worst" and to go for it while you're young and able to, and I'm glad I decided to take those leaps of faith just a few short years ago. Nothing I could have done would have prepared me for the wild ride that would unfold as a result of me showing up, being present, and trusting the universe and its processes.

While I'm going to keep it fairly positive, some of the learning lessons and stories I'm going to share might not make sense to you. Still to this day, at times they don't even make sense to me, but there is no straight arrow road in life to the mountaintop. Anyone and everyone you know of or that you've heard of doing something meaningful had to zig-zag on their journey, as even the "overnight successes" had to do something beforehand to put themselves in a position to be ready when their moment came. I by no means am an overnight success, and I'm still not entirely comfortable saying that I'm "successful," as there's still a lot more work that needs to be done with the projects in which I'm involved to have them sustain long term generational success. But I can tell you with pride and a smile that I'm continuing to establish myself in this world by getting one step closer to the mountaintop than I was the day before, and I'm two steps closer than I was the day before that, and continually trekking my way up the *mountain* in this journey called **life**.

Learning Lesson

In the previous chapter I asked what interests and hobbies do you have? Now that you've hopefully identified some, do you have a passion others might share? Or an idea lying inside of you that you've always thought you should share with the world? Have you considered starting a blog, a social media page, or an outlet to share more information about it? How about joining a meetup group with other like-minded individuals who might share this same passion? I've found that sharing ideas with others can have a profound impact not only on your own life, but the lives of others around you. What if you are just one idea, one spark, one connection away from changing the world you live in? As you'll come to find out, this initial idea of blogging, then food blogging, then arts & culture blogging and starting Choose954 led to many other ideas that might never have come to life had I not shared them with others. Maybe your world-changing ideas are around the corner, or the next block, or the next street, or the next town over—if you put them out into the universe. I encourage you to spread your light, your mission, and your "why" with others before it's too late for you to look back at a missed opportunity. Amazing things happen outside of your comfort zone, and happen as a result of showing up, being present, and trusting the universe with its processes.

Chapter 5

Learning To Choose Psilocybin And Boiler Room

"Taking LSD (psychedelics) was a profound experience, one of the most important things in my life. (Psychedelics) show you that there's another side to the coin, and you can't remember it when it wears off, but you know it. It reinforced my sense of what was important – creating great things instead of making money, putting things back into the stream of history and of human consciousness as much as I could." —**Steve Jobs, co-founder of Apple, pioneer of the personal computer era**

As I've previously alluded to, there are a few special people in my life who have come along and have shown me amazing things. One person I'm eternally grateful for and worth reiterating is my friend and former roommate "Lefty". Before I knew what path I was on, or what a path in life really was, Lefty was well on his own path. He was an explorer, a journey-er, and was on his path to seeing how far the consciousness rabbit hole would go before I ever knew what these terms meant. I would come to find through my initial adventures to Wynwood in 2014-2015 with Lefty that on this path, there were very uniquely curated experiences in the form of music events featuring some of the best **House DJ's** in the world who would frequently play their tunes throughout the *Miami scene*. It had been quite a few years since I had experienced anything like this firsthand, and I was blown away by what I discovered.

In my senior year of high school in 2004, I had been to one underground rave event (DJ Icey's "Candyland") with blaring drum and bass techno music, nostalgic TV screens looping old cartoon scenes, very indicative of what you'll find in a history book regarding the rave culture of the 1990s and 2000s. I understand this might not resonate with all readers, but I ask you to bear with me even if this is unfamiliar, as this type of dance music is internationally regarded as a leading genre and a major component of international culture. If you don't pick up those history books and can use an additional reference to visualize what I'm attempting to illustrate, it would be reminiscent of what you might find in a documentary about the 1980s *Limelight* clubs in New York City, but with an early 2000s South Florida spin. Though this scene I was beginning to discover in 2015 was much, much different. There was a more mature element to the partygoers and people you would find on the dance floor. The very nature of house music was that of having slower **BPMs** (beats per minute) than the previously more up beat *techno music* that you would associate with "Ultra Music Festival" or a party where there's *fist pumping* going on. While you would find very diverse people of all ages and varying backgrounds/cross sections of life here, everyone seemed to get along and jive naturally over and through the music; there were never really any major fights like you would find at traditional clubs. Everyone seemed to love the music, love each other, and love life while dancing the night away to these **funky house beats**. These early music experiences laid the groundwork for me to appreciate a new level of experiences soon to come, which would change my outlook on music and experiential events altogether.

If you've made it thus far into the book, I take it you have some appreciation for the work I'm doing personally and professionally, which I genuinely appreciate. I know this next chapter might be met with a little bit of skepticism, and somehow I waited to write this chapter last which led to the current state of affairs we're living in upon this books publication in 2023, where what I'm about to expand upon is becoming socially acceptable after decades of being stigmatized. But what I am about to explain can truly not be described simply with words—it has to be experienced and it has to be felt for you to truly understand the impact (if you haven't already). But for the sake of sharing my story I will do my best to express the impact with words and references you hopefully will come to comprehend and appreciate.

I was always secretly a seeker of experiences whether I knew it or not. Be it sports games, trips and adventures, or even nature, I enjoyed exploring the unknown and the realms/depths of what I could safely experience. It was in this period of exploration into the arts and culture in 2014-2015, shortly after I moved in with my roommate, that Lefty introduced me to two things that would profoundly shape my life—at the same time. As I was beginning to develop my love for house music, a *"plant"* in the form of **medicine** was introduced to me which inherently produced a more prolific experience than anything I had experienced prior. The **plant medicine** I'm referring to is psilocybin, otherwise known as "magic mushrooms." Still uncertain about where I'm going with this? Bear with me for a moment while I explain with some references.

A little background that I feel is worth mentioning to provide greater context. "Psilocybin[1] (/ˌsaɪləˈsaɪbɪn/ sy-lə-SY-bin) is a naturally occurring psychedelic compound produced by more than 200 species of fungi. ... Imagery found on prehistoric murals and rock paintings of modern-day Spain and Algeria suggests that human usage of psilocybin mushrooms predates recorded history.

Some of the key benefits associated with psilocybin include:[2]

---

[1] Wikipedia. "Psilocybin." Wikipedia, https://en.wikipedia.org/wiki/Psilocybin
[2] https://theplantmedicinepath.com/psilocybin/

1. Enhanced Mood and Reduced Depression: Psilocybin has been shown to have antidepressant effects, offering relief for individuals struggling with depression. It can lead to a sense of heightened well-being, improved mood, and increased emotional openness.

2. Anxiety and Stress Reduction: Psilocybin has demonstrated the ability to alleviate anxiety and reduce stress levels. It can help individuals confront and process deep-rooted fears and anxieties, leading to long-lasting reductions in anxiety symptoms.

3. Increased Mindfulness and Spiritual Connection: Psilocybin has been described as a tool for facilitating profound spiritual experiences and promoting a sense of interconnectedness. It can enhance feelings of mindfulness, transcendence, and a connection to something larger than oneself.

4. Improved Creativity and Cognitive Flexibility: Studies have suggested that psilocybin may enhance creativity and cognitive flexibility. It can lead to unconventional thinking, novel problem-solving approaches, and increased openness to new ideas.

5. Addiction Treatment Support: Psilocybin has shown promise in the treatment of various addictions, including tobacco, alcohol, and substance use disorders. It can help

individuals gain new perspectives, break destructive patterns, and experience a sense of spiritual renewal.

6. Enhanced Emotional Resilience: Psilocybin-assisted therapy has demonstrated the potential to increase emotional resilience and improve coping mechanisms. It can assist individuals in processing past traumas, fostering self-compassion, and promoting psychological growth.

7. Palliative Care and End-of-Life Support: Psilocybin has been explored as a means of providing psychological and existential support to individuals facing terminal illnesses. It can help alleviate end-of-life anxiety, provide a sense of peace, and facilitate a more meaningful perspective on life and mortality.

8. It is important to note that psilocybin should be used in a controlled and therapeutic setting, preferably under the guidance of trained professionals, if not at home in a safe space. Research into psilocybin's benefits is ongoing, and further studies are necessary to fully understand its potential and optimize its application.

In Mesoamerica, the mushrooms had long been consumed in spiritual and divinatory ceremonies before Spanish chroniclers first documented their use in the sixteenth century." It is argued, and otherwise now almost confirmed, that psilocybin mushrooms helped us evolve as a species to the human beings we've become today, a development commonly referred to as "The stoned ape theory." First proposed by the legendary 20th century ethnobotanist Terence McKenna (1946-2000) in his 1992 book *Food of the Gods*, the basic concept is that the consumption of psychedelic fungi may have played a crucial role in the **development of human minds, brains, and culture.** In essence, the hypothesis suggests we owe the emergence of language and self-reflection to ancient, sustained consumption of psilocybin mushrooms. The exact timeline for the emergence of consciousness varies, but Terence's brother Dennis McKenna, one of the most respected ethnopharmacologists and research pharmacognosists of our time, believes the process may have begun as far back as 2 million years ago.

"We know the brain tripled in size about 2 million years ago, and probably the ecosystems which put hominids, cattle and mushrooms together were around that old," Terrence McKenna's brother Dennis says, referring to the dung from which psilocybin mushrooms emerge.

According to Dr. Thomas Falk, a professor of Philosophy and Education at the University of Dayton, the hypothesis also provides an explanation for the so-called **"creative explosion"** that occurred *40,000 years ago in homo sapiens, prior to their* *migration from Africa to Europe.* It is here that we see an apparent leap in **human cognitive ability.**

"For the first time ever, these humans lived in worlds of their own creation, materially and symbolically," Falk says via email. "Like you and I, these humans were capable of creating worlds in their heads and then re-creating those worlds in the external physical and social environments. Although other homo species may have efficiently exploited nature, they remained its passive subjects. The key to this major distinction between homo sapiens and all other hominids appears to be *language*."

In his book *Food of the Gods*, McKenna argues that due to desertification in Africa, humans retreated to the shrinking tropical forests, following cattle herds whose dung attracted the insects that he states were certainly a part of the human diet at the time. According to his hypothesis, humans would have detected Psilocybe cubensis (mushrooms) from this due to it often growing in cowpats.

According to McKenna, access to and ingestion of mushrooms was an evolutionary advantage to humans' omnivorous hunter-gatherer ancestors, also providing humanity's first religious impulse. He believed that psilocybin mushrooms were the "evolutionary catalyst" from which language, projective imagination, the arts, religion, philosophy, science, and all of human culture sprang.

The effects of psilocybin are highly variable and depend on the mindset and environment in which the user has the experience, factors commonly referred to as **set and setting.**

One of the most fascinating things I want to share regarding these medicinal mushrooms is their ability to increase *neuroplasticity,* which is the brain's ability to change and adapt to external stimuli over time. This includes neuronal death, neurogenesis (new neurons), creating new neural pathways and synaptic connections. Why is it beneficial to increase neuroplasticity? Neuroplasticity is associated with learning, new experiences, and memory formation. The more efficiently the brain is able to create new neurons and new synaptic connections, the better we are able to perform these tasks. It can also benefit those with neurological disorders. Magic mushrooms are thought to increase your brain's neuroplasticity via the 5HT1A serotonin receptor. In rodent studies, it has increased the rate of neurogenesis in the hippocampus and prefrontal cortex. Scientists are truly just scratching the surface on the research of what these medicinal mushrooms are capable of accomplishing, but for the sake of this story I'll share some of how they've been impactful for me.

For my first experience, easily one of the most significant experiences of my life until this point, I found myself in our apartment with three friends eating a chocolate concoction embedded with the psilocybin mushroom that you couldn't taste. Around forty-five minutes thereafter I began to feel positive effects in my mind and body come on unlike anything which I had ever experienced before in my life. While the feelings of euphoria, one-ness with the world, and open-mindedness were building within the first hour, they quickly became accentuated by Lefty going over to the desktop computer towards the office space of our apartment and putting on some music I had never heard before. These sounds, entering into my eardrums at what would be a serendipitous time of my life, undoubtedly changed the way I viewed music and experiences thereafter.

The YouTube channel he pulled up was called **Boiler Room**, and the *DJ Set* as they are referred to was from a British Vinyl DJ who goes by the moniker **Nightmares On Wax**. The way I understood it, Boiler Room was an up-and-coming movement from London, UK where a group of house music lovers brought in some of the top house music DJs in the world to host intimate music listening experiences (oftentimes parties). What made it popular in my eyes was that they would stream these experiences with a new dynamic POV camera setup highlighting the DJ playing the music and accentuating the crowd in the background to set the tone and vibe for the epic video replays. This very first set I experienced listening to had a very nostalgic sound, playing old R&B/soul classics on vinyl mixed with a modern 2013 vibe (at the time it was released). The experience was recorded in what appeared to be an old missile silo, a sphere/curved roof structure donned with pictures of culture-laden memories and flags from islands I had dreamt of visiting one day in the background. The DJ was setting the very relatable vibes while vibing out himself, with the dozen or so attendees who sat behind him swirling in conversation which slowly led to head nodding in appreciation of the music they were there to experience.

I was simultaneously falling in love with watching this experience as my senses were heightened while thoroughly enjoying the music and camaraderie amongst my friends. In our apartment, the small group of us who had consumed the mushrooms huddled around the computer, and while the effects of the mushrooms were kicking in, I found it truly piqued our curiosity in an exuberant and playful manner. We found what appeared to be much joy in asking each other, "Where are they? How did they get there? Who are these people in the background? How do you get tickets to something like this?" as this music experience lasted just under ninety minutes.

It was the wonder and mystique of this newfound experience, coupled with what I can describe as my first of many "mystical experiences," that I instantly fell in love with. I immediately mentally bookmarked this Boiler Room concept, and subsequently in the days after the mushroom experience dove down the rabbit hole of what I could find on YouTube for more. They were initially happening on rooftops on flats in London, and then in Brooklyn, and occasionally in exotic places like Ibiza and Tulum. While the level of DJs they were bringing to curate the sounds and vibes for these experiences was truly world-class, it was the scene—including the **people-watching** in the background—that set the vibe, making watching these video replays even more magical versus just listening. I started realizing and appreciating how this Boiler Room concept was shaping house music culture globally, and became more and more drawn to this art form called *house music*.

Not many people outside of my close friends know this, but it was this burgeoning love for house music, fueled by my newfound *plant medicine journey* expanding my consciousness, that led me deeper down the path of pursuing arts and culture after initially discovering this new found world through blogging and my III Points/Wynwood experiences. As I was settling into a new life in the evolving Downtown Fort Lauderdale scene, I found a bug—a calling of sorts to recreate this magic in my community. Fortunately, one of my friends and mentors, **Juan**, also had a love for house music, and despite being a successful retail management executive, he happened to thoroughly enjoy DJing on the side for fun. It was recultivating this love for playing music for our friends that got Juan back on the DJ decks, and soon led to us trying to create our own "Boiler Room vibes" on the fourth floor rooftop pool deck in the Downtown Fort Lauderdale building we had recently moved into. The rooftop deck fortunately had a beautiful backdrop scene of the city's evolving skyline, which would provide the closest taste of the Boiler Room experience our community would ever see.

"All we wanted was a little house music" was what we would say. We thought if we played it, the people–even just our neighbors and friends, would come. This subsequently began a series of pool parties at our building with other local DJ friends where great conversations and connections were established as I was now establishing myself in Downtown Fort Lauderdale. After a few of these events at our building, we slowly started forming a group of like-minded, music-loving individuals who were starting to meet up at a local co-working space to brainstorm ideas of how to create a music scene in our beloved community.

This was actually my first real community building venture, before Choose954, to **try and build a house music scene in Fort Lauderdale**. I was hopeful, and maybe a bit optimistic at the time, that we could build a "cool enough" culture to warrant the curators behind Boiler Room to host an event with us instead of Miami or other major cities they would travel to for these events. Somehow, I consciously recognized shortly into this endeavor that building a house music scene in my community on its own was an uphill battle, and one I did not have the resources to fight. Booking big name DJs to fly into town would take a lot of money, money at this point I did not have. However, I was able to pivot this mission into my broader arts and culture endeavors, and was able to integrate DJs playing house music into the events we began producing, starting with Juan playing our initial events for free to support the movement.

While we never ended up getting Boiler Room to come, I do believe the elevation of the conversation, if nothing else, led to a rise in the desire for more house music in our community, making way for future events and movements which did contribute to the cultural landscape of Fort Lauderdale. To clarify, I by no means am taking credit for the work my contemporaries, peers, and friends did in the Broward County area as it relates to producing house music events. I was truly glad to support the pop-up events, pool parties, and the few clubs that were playing house music at that time as I saw the impact this had globally in places like Berlin, London, and Ibiza. After being inspired by this quote, I used to often say, "**Support comes in many different ways, but one of the best ways to support the community is to show up to other people's stuff.**" I'd like to think by showing up and supporting we helped move the needle forward, and changed a few lives in the process.

Many positive results came out of this initial experience of discovering Boiler Room and Psilocybin, but one of the more noteworthy success stories worth sharing from these experiences is about a music producer friend. This friend had previously experienced a successful run earlier in life as a DJ, making it all the way to play on a stage at a major music festival out west before moving out east and settling into a much quieter life in his thirties. As we were beginning the brainstorming conversations locally, we discovered a meetup for DJs in Midtown Miami held at a Five Guys that piqued our interest enough to go explore, and after urging him multiple times to join Juan and myself to see what this was all about, our friend (Nico, aka "Stanley Kubrix") decided to join us.

It was at this meeting of maybe twenty or so DJs and producers that Nico and I connected with a handful of guys who also lived in Broward and had made the trip, and who were trying to create a similar movement with electronic music, though more on the harder side of the beats with genres called trance and "dubstep." I can't take the credit for the rest of the story, but lo and behold, despite being somewhat introverted by his own admission, Nico formed many friendships as a result of attending this initial meetup, which re-engaged him more in the local music scene in Fort Lauderdale that he had not previously been a part of. After slowly coming out of his shell to attend some local music events, and ultimately playing music at them (including our pool parties), Nico had a resurgence in his music career. This resurgence led to him pursuing music again full time, moving back to the Los Angeles area of California where he was originally from and where he had more opportunities to pursue his craft.

He has since gone on to successfully produce a catalog of his own music as well as music for noteworthy artists, reaching the tops of some of the most prestigious charts in the electronic dance music industry, and has played music at some of the coolest venues in L.A. and on the West Coast. I love to joke with Nico and our mutual friends, saying, "Aren't you glad you decided to get off the couch that day and join us at Five Guys?" Years later it still brings a smile to our faces, as I am grateful to have played a small role in changing this friend's life for the better—one of the things I now realize fills my cup more than anything else.

Being there, supporting others, lifting up my friends and members of my community to be their best and pursue their dreams and goals gives me my oxygen and keeps me going. This is just another friendly reminder that anything is possible, and if you put your head down to grind hard working on your passion, you too can pursue your dreams to the point they become a profession and don't feel like **work**.

As for the magic mushrooms, I am proud to announce that in the current state of affairs at the time of publishing this book, that psilocybin mushrooms have reached a renaissance and are getting the recognition they deserve for their healing abilities. What used to be a purely underground or taboo subject for most is now being discussed regularly on the top health and wellness podcast of the moment (The Huberman Lab, highly recommended) as well as the #1 listened to podcasts around the world (The Joe Rogan Experience, also highly recommended). Rightfully so, these medicinal mushrooms are now being fast tracked by legislators and the FDA for legalization as a result of their therapeutic properties, primarily for helping people overcome alcoholism, depression, PTSD, as well as helping cancer patients and various people cope after receiving a terminal diagnosis with a new perspective on life. It's often referred to in psychedelic literature and research that as little as one *session* with the mushrooms, with the right "*set and setting*", can generate the same impacts (or greater) than those experienced after years of therapy. While I haven't been to therapy since I was an adolescent giving my parents a tough time, I have dealt with quite a bit of highs and lows internally that I needed to address. Be it things not working out with women as I had hoped that crushed my hopes and dreams, or the loss of friends to cancer, or partnerships that didn't work out for various reasons–I found much internal solace and healing in my psilocybin *ceremonies*, as I refer to them. For the record, I only embark on these **journeys** in the comfort of my own home, the majority of the time by myself for my own *internal research and development purposes* with the ideal **set and setting**, which any experienced "voyager" or trained therapist will tell you is the most vital component. Set refers to the state of mind you are in when going inwards, while setting means where you are—preferably comfortable in your own surroundings with minimal distractions, as your mind expands to new levels and dimensions. As you can witness in Michael Pollens' *How to Change Your Mind* Netflix series and New York Times bestselling book, it is recommended to **go inward** by laying down, with headphones and eyeshades on, to process whatever *comes up for you* through the medicine.

I am proud to share that this **work** has led to incredible levels of growth, which I attribute to being truly one of the most impactful tools I've ever had in my tool kit. While these journeys are not all rainbows and unicorns in the process of going inward to address life's toughest challenges, the comfort and reassurance I found from the messages I've received which let me know everything would be okay have become one of my strongest guiding principles. I've processed some of the most glorious moments of my life and some of the toughest depths of despair through the mushrooms, and undoubtedly have come out better as a result. Be it business ventures and relationships not working out as intended, to the untimely loss of friends and loved ones, the comforting medicine I turned to in the form of plants were there for me when I needed them. While it might not be something you would traditionally consider helpful, these moments in my life have been one of my most beloved forms of self-care. Some of my most profound ideas, brainstorm sessions, and recollections have come from the mushrooms. Honestly, I more than likely would not be sitting here writing this in 2023 if not for the mushrooms, let alone having developed into the human being I've become whose writing this book you are now reading.

I wrestled internally about including this chapter in the book over the last two years of writing it, but finally felt this is something I feel comfortable sharing and am glad to discuss further if it's of interest to you as the reader to reach out to me. Thanks to great work being done over the last few decades from the likes of the good people at Johns Hopkins University and MAPS (Multidisciplinary Association for Psychedelic Studies), it is looking promising that in the next few years these medicinal mushrooms will be rescheduled, controlled, and administered for therapeutic use. Actually, it is currently slated to happen in the state of Oregon later this year (2023), and has already happened in various progressive countries across the globe. There is endless positive insight and hopeful speculation on the potential out there, but it is widely concluded from anyone who has experimented and had a positive experience that these compounds truly do have the potential to provide a **renaissance in mental health care**, which could lead to a much needed evolution in the psyche of our society.

Now that you read this, does it all still seem so scary to you? I'm not here to address how the government's war on drugs and the media has cloaked these medicinal mushrooms with fear mongering and scare tactics, but I encourage you to do your own research to deduce your own conclusion. Of course, I am not a doctor and I am not advising you to do anything in particular, aside from considering all of the options available when assessing your own unique situation in life.

Learning Lesson

What types of things do you do for your self-care? Or to go inward and reflect upon your life? Have you tried new things that have actively opened your mind to new peaks and valleys you previously never explored - like holotropic breathing? When was the last time you explored a new music genre, or musical experience? While I realize that Boiler Room and psilocybin mushrooms are not for everyone, I want you to consider stepping outside of your comfort zone to see what new levels of growth you can find. Maybe it's through yoga or a form of meditation? Or ecstatic dance at a "silent disco" party? Or a form of exercise that helps you reach a heightened state like "runner's high." By opening new neural pathways in your mind, you might just find a paradigm shift in your life you didn't know you needed or even that you wanted on the other side.

CHAPTER 6

Learning To Choose A Business Partner

"That's Never Going To Happen…" - **Evan Snow, Said Before Some Epic Things That We Eventually Made Happen**

I can't say I started this journey with nothing; I was very, very fortunate to have great parents who were VERY patient with me through my teenage years. Despite me doing almost everything to the contrary of what they would have wanted me to do in the earlier stages in my life (sorry, Mom and Dad), they loved me unconditionally and knew to let me learn from my mistakes.

As I got into my late twenties and was really becoming a man, I was fortunate to connect with and befriend some amazing people who recognized my potential. First, a mutual friend and retail management executive, Juan, with whom I shared many interests. Being a good friend and mentor who knew my love for TEDtalks, Juan invited me to the monthly breakfast lecture series (CM), and subsequently initiated entrepreneurial conversations that pushed me and inevitably many others in our circle of friends to do more in life.

But above and beyond everyone else, I truly wouldn't be writing this had I not met one of the most ingenious, altruistic, generous, and creative people in the world who fortunately was in the right place at the right time wanting to impact our community—my business partner, Mr. Andrew Martineau. When I met Andrew I had just started Choose954 after dabbling in food blogging and taking my first trip to Memphis, Tennessee for the World Championship BBQ Festival. Little did I know the path that would be in front of me as a result of this chance encounter.

2016 was the year for me - I learned how to choose to be an entrepreneur & community builder

One skill I fortunately acquired earlier on in life and developed through my recruiting experience was that of **networking**. I've always had a good way of making conversations relatable, somehow always knowing how to connect dots when they weren't so clear, and thankfully was likable enough that people gravitated towards sharing (and oftentimes over sharing) with me while out at events. In February 2016 I attended my first CM event after my pivotal "aha moment" the previous month at Broward College's downtown campus, where I met a lawyer/professor named Natalie Butto. Natalie had an incredible background.

She had attended Georgetown University, hosted radio shows, was corporate counsel for huge Fortune 500 companies, taught entrepreneurship classes, facilitated retreats, and somehow took a liking to me upon meeting that fateful February morning. Fast forward a few months later, I began running into Natalie at more and more events as I was going around town, and we developed a friendship based around our shared interests of entrepreneurship and community building—two of my budding passions. I came to find out that Natalie taught an Entrepreneurship Capstone class at Broward College, and somehow she knew I had potential inside of me I didn't know I had in myself.

When I was invited by Natalie to the Tower Club in downtown Fort Lauderdale for the first time, I could never have imagined how much my life would change from that one evening. The invitation was for a TED Simulcast event where she played Amanda Palmer's TED Talk on 'The Art Of Asking' - one of the top 10 watched talks of all time on YouTube (at the time), and moderated some thought-provoking conversation afterwards before leaving the attendees to mix and mingle. The way the story goes is, after the talk I was sharing with an old gray-haired guy to my right about this Choose954 thing I was firecharged about and had just started at the artwalk the month prior. As I came to find out later and won't get into so much detail throughout this book in an effort to keep things positive, he really could have cared less.

This was in part because it didn't appear, as it didn't appear to many old gray-haired people in Fort Lauderdale, that this Choose954 thing could immediately benefit their business or even their community.

Well thankfully, on the other side of me to my left, there was a very sharply dressed Trinidadian fellow with a Dali mustache and an intense focus who was sitting at the same table and overheard what I had to say. He initially sat there quietly, and after the conversation I was having fizzled, he began taking an interest in speaking with me. He was ten years my senior and in part, was very similar to me ten years earlier in life I came to find out as it related to art and community building. Somehow, after just a few minutes of chatting, he invited me to join him for a coffee meeting there at the Tower Club the following week. At this time I had recently left recruiting for the first time to *pursue my passions*, which for full transparency means I really had no idea what I was doing or where I was going. I was dabbling in things like blogging, selling Google My Business Listing services to local businesses with a friend/neighbor, but ultimately my main source of income came from rideshare driving Uber and Lyft. While it's not something I was proud about doing, I was able to set my own hours, I was able to do and see the things I wanted to see within the arts and culture, which I was feverishly exploring at that time. But more importantly, I was able to meet

Andrew for coffee midmorning without having a boss at an office I needed to lie to, saying I was "meeting a prospective client" as a reason for not being at my desk.

I will never forget that first meeting with Andrew at the Tower Club. He was dressed sharply in one of his Zara suits with his "money bag" (expensive leather backpack), and looked at me with a stare like he was peering into my soul. He must have been peering into my soul, as he inevitably saw something in me that I truly did not know existed. I can vividly remember early on in the conversation it started with me going first, running down my brief resume of the adult work experience I had compiled – starting in a call center as an outbound sales representative, rising to sales manager at twenty-one years old in my first job. This led to me working for an AT&T authorized retailer selling cell phones, which led to me transitioning to Verizon Wireless corporate retail sales in an effort to pursue climbing the corporate ladder. After I lost interest in selling cell phones and retail sales, I began dabbling in residential real estate with my uncle while playing poker semi-professionally, which ultimately led to friends encouraging me to get into the "staffing industry" as a recruiter. I do attribute that experience to teaching me how to fit a square peg in a round hole and connect dots for companies of various sizes, including how to do so on an enterprise organization level.

Andrew's resume and experience absolutely blew me away, as he humbly said he "wanted to be an artist, but liked nice things–so he couldn't be a full time artist and got into advertising/marketing". He had come to this country from Trinidad to go to art school at the International Fine Arts College (IFAC, now called Miami University Of Art & Design), where he had digital art pioneer Laurence Gartel as a college professor, taught art to the youth at the Turner Guilford Knight Correctional Center (jail in Miami), and worked for some of the top advertising agencies early on including Satchi/JWT. Andrew gained experience doing advertising and creative campaigns for the likes of Gulfstream Park, Royal Caribbean, and most of the housing communities being developed in South Florida in the early 2000's including GL Homes and other respected builders. He developed the logo still used to this day by the Las Olas Association, split office space with Tony Cho of Metro1 in the early days of Wynwood, one of the leading commercial real estate brokers at the time who in part responsible for contributing the increase in leasing and development activity prior to the "Wynwood Effect". Andrew had attended art school with the likes of Brandon Opalka and other great Miami artists with whom he would chip in on the rent of a warehouse studio in Wynwood for $100 a month at the time. Fast forward a few years and those same warehouses would now sell for

$40,000,000+. Quick history lesson: Do you know how that happened? Do you know why that was the case? **It was because of the arts.**

Andrew had since moved to Fort Lauderdale a few years prior to us meeting and developed a love for the Broward County community, having contributed to moving countless initiatives forward in his previous iteration of community building efforts prior to me knowing community building was even a thing I should be advocating for. But thankfully above all of that, we shared a love of art and supporting artists, which for me was really just flourishing at this time.

After moving to Broward County he became involved with our local American Advertising Federation (AAF) chapter for which he's now supported for over 20 years serving as past president multiple times. In addition to AAF Andrew spent considerable time sitting on various Chamber Of Commerce boards, membership organizations, and was a driver in the early days of the "Creative Economy" conversation. He contributed to numerous county initiatives including The Broward Centennial celebration, the "Vision 2020" plan, the creation of FAT Village + Las Olas Art Walks, the Art As An Entrepreneur Institute (AEI), and found time to support the local Film Commission. Fortunately and unfortunately he had a business partner with whom he built the first coworking and multi-functional space in Broward County called the "Collide Factory" in FAT Village (which later became the home of C&I Studios), who up and left in the middle of the night without paying the rent. This series of events in part led to Andrew getting frustrated with the rate and pace of change being made at the time in Broward County, which without having a business partner to support him on this journey ultimately drove him to going back to working in the "corporate world".

When we met he was still a Regional Marketing Director with the Westfield Corporation—one of the largest mall operators in the world. Looking back on it now, it was those unfortunate experiences, the highs and lows, that somehow mysteriously led him to me and our future partnership. As a result of these experiences Andrew knew a lot of the behind-the-scenes players, drama, letdowns, shady stories, and disappointments within city and county government in our community. I was blind to these facts and many others that wouldn't make the newspaper, having grown up in the suburb of Coral Springs where there seemed to not be so much political drama on my radar.

It was these facts, and so many others, that fortunately Andrew was able to share with me as insight, market knowledge, best practices, tips and tricks, and countless other nuggets of information no book and ultimately no one else would have or could have shared with me. I could go on for days and days with gratitude which he doesn't need to hear me recount in this chapter, but undoubtedly above anyone else or any other story I could possibly tell, I would not be sitting here writing this book without the support of my business partner and friend, Mr. Andrew Martineau. While there was a clear gap in experience, we both shared a similar uncanny drive and desire for something more for our city, community, and the world — which I still haven't found in anyone else I have met since then. Before I knew it was a thing, Andrew taught me about a word that would become one of my guiding principles: **altruism**, which I interpreted as *genuinely doing something good in the world without holding your hand out expecting something in return*. Andrew found ways to bestow this on me to give us an underlying foundation necessary to do community building work we would go on to do — which oftentimes would be thankless, doing things behind the scenes that most people never see, hear of, or even appreciate. It was becoming apparent to me that fortunately Andrew was at a point of his life where he could mentor, befriend, and partner with me to do greater things in our community—together. At first we weren't sure what those things would be, but we continued meeting for coffee weekly, until our third coffee meeting which changed everything.

Around this time, the Art Basel fair in Miami Beach had become one of the most desired destinations for art annually in the first week of December, which served as a huge catalyst for change in Miami just a few minutes south of us in Fort Lauderdale. Artists, collectors, gallerists, and celebrities would flock from all over the world initially to see and purchase the art, and attend lavish parties. This recipe led to the annual art fair becoming a place where people would get dressed up to "see and be seen," contributing to the ever evolving culture in Miami and some exceptional people-watching opportunities. But more importantly, this series of events that primarily took place at the Miami Beach convention center and eventually spread throughout the city was a huge economic driver for the local economy and the art market. Every year the press was reporting on the economic impact, the home sales, the companies that were moving to Miami, and all of the other perks that came as a result of this thing they call *Art Basel*. There is no way to properly calculate the economic impact between local, national, and international visitors – but it is speculated that over *one million people* attend the various events that surround the week of Art Basel, and that those attendees contribute over **one billion dollars** to the local economy between their various purchases (including art and real estate).

We never really had anything like this in Broward County. Sure, we have the longest running boat show in the world (with a reported $800,000,000+ economic impact), but that really only caters to a certain audience and wasn't something that everyone enjoyed attending. There were some "art fairs" in the streets and in parking lots throughout our community, but they were generally repetitive and weren't anything that celebrities were flying in for or that people would flock to in their artsy attire. There truly was a void, and a need, for something greater in the community. I thought one day early on, in my infinite wisdom, that we would call this *Basel In Broward*. Fortunately, Andrew also shared this desire for a greater platform in our community to not only highlight and showcase the talented local artists of whom we wanted to be supportive, but to create something that would "put Fort Lauderdale on the art world map as an international destination to view and interact with art." So it was there, at that table in the Tower Club, within the first few weeks of even knowing him, that we ideated what would become **Art Fort Lauderdale - "The Art Fair On The Water." (Which I will go on to explain in the next chapter)**

We have since changed our community, the art fair world, and ultimately a portion of the world overall for the better through the gifts and platforms we innovated to bring to our community and beyond. I hope the history books, not just this history book, give credit where credit is due because none of this would have happened without the support of the ingeniousness/ingenuity of Andrew Martineau, aka "**The Creative Altruist.**"

Learning Lesson

I know everyone has their own unique situation—kids, family, life—but if you have an opportunity to "go for it" while you are still young, I strongly encourage you to do so. Looking back on it, I probably didn't go about my entrepreneurial journey the most optimal way possible, living in an expensive apartment in Downtown Fort Lauderdale, driving Uber longer than I should have while putting more miles on my car than I needed to. But it was all of those experiences, seeing all of the things I wanted to go see and do, that led me to the person I am today. **Do you have people in your life helping you move forward? Or is there one person too many that's holding you back? Do you know where in your community you can tap into like-minded, bigger picture thinkers with whom you can ideate and collaborate?** Whether you're just getting started on your entrepreneurial journey or you are already an established business owner, I encourage you to seek them out as we all have something to learn and something to give back.

Chapter 7

Learning To Choose A Venture (Art Fort Lauderdale - "The Art Fair On The Water")

"Hardships Often Prepare Ordinary People For An Extraordinary Destiny" - **C.S. Lewis**

While sitting at a table near the window in the Tower Club overlooking all of Broward County in one of our first initial meetings, Andrew and I concluded there were a few things missing from our community's cultural landscape that needed to be addressed. The lack of these platforms, we felt, created an opportunity for us to fill these voids with new and innovative concepts that could help immediately catapult our efforts into the limelight in a short period of time. We thought, "What can we do to differentiate ourselves from all of the other art fairs in the world?" which were held traditionally in tents, convention centers, and hotels. We realized Fort Lauderdale has unique elements of which many people are aware, but they weren't exactly being highlighted in ways that locals would enjoy, let alone prompt someone from another part of the world to fly in and experience. The city boasts an intracoastal waterway system with miles of winding canals that lead to the inlet and the ocean. Beautiful homes (mansions) line the "Venice Of The

Americas," with stunning architecture and boat docks; Fort Lauderdale is one of the few cities with a water taxi system that can transport people on the water instead of just on land.

Furthermore, the art fair model was crying out for reinventing at this time—quite literally. A recent article in one of the top art publications affirmed the *art world's* consensus of yearning for something more than the large mazes art patrons would find upon entering the "signature art fairs" that took place throughout the world. These four-day fairs filled convention halls with rows of white walls making up booths where galleries would pay exorbitant amounts of money to show a few pieces of art, which unfortunately provided a large barrier of entry for independent artists to participate. If only successful galleries could exhibit in these fairs, and if our local artists didn't have platforms through which they could be discovered, supported, and collected to garner gallerists' attentions, how were any of these artists we were befriending supposed to make it to that "next level" to advance in their artistic career? We thought to ourselves, there has to be a better way.

This is where the idea for Art Fort Lauderdale, The Art Fair On The Water (ArtFTL) was born. After flushing out the initial concept, we were confident that the city, the tourism board, the business community, and other various stakeholders in the county would hop on board full force to support this. We had seen event concepts without the unique novelty of ArtFTL boast dozens of sponsors on their flyers, something generally necessary to underwrite and produce large scale productions like a multi-day art fair.

Well, you would think if someone told you they were inventing a new concept to revolutionize the art world by hosting an art fair held inside luxury waterfront homes, which were off of the Las Olas Intracoastal Waterways made only accessible via boat, that influential stakeholders and decision makers within the community would gravitate towards it. One would think…

In a town I can only summarize as "not being savvy" or very progressive with the arts and culture, for lack of a better term, unfortunately, the gravitation did not happen at the rate it should or could have.

At this point in 2016, I had recently begun supporting the arts through cultural curation with Choose954, covering artists and arts districts that didn't necessarily have the money or means to market themselves. The monetization path of this venture was not clear at this time, and I quickly realized this was something no one really had an objective or requirement to do—especially with continual cuts to newspapers, magazines, and arts writing. I started doing this work initially because I felt a calling to do so, and accelerated these efforts "because it was the right thing to do" shortly after finding out from Andrew what *altruism* really was. Little did I know that "doing good without having your hand out expecting anything in return" (my interpretation of altruism) would lead me down a path that I'm not saying was the darkest of times, but it certainly wasn't paved with gold. This path involved many sleepless nights, recurring bouts of feeling bitter/jaded, a stretch of driving Uber and Lyft for over a year to make ends meet, which inevitably led me back to the recruiting world I had left to join "entrepreneurville." This might be a good time to tell you about a mental complex I found out about that persisted in the community: unfortunately, a good majority of the stakeholders who were in a position to support efforts like ours were more content with "turning their heads and looking the other way, hoping things would get better," which was not a recipe for success.

Spoiler alert, things did not initially get better, and they only started to slowly improve as **we learned to choose** to do it on our own. I can hear David Goggins in my head now, wishing I would have heard him back then, saying, "No one is coming to save you." He was right, and these people were content with letting us fail, or with letting us float while we did what we said we were setting out to do—**putting Fort Lauderdale on the art**

world map as an international destination to view and interact with art. Period. That was the goal, that was the mission, and thankfully my newfound business partner was committed to making this happen. Andrew was so convinced this possibility was a reality, that when it became apparent we weren't going to receive the funding necessary to underwrite the behind-the-scenes cost of producing the event—including chartering water taxis, marketing, and everything else it takes to bring an idea to life—he decided to fund it, himself. So as the story goes, my business partner, who had recently left a comfortable position as a marketing director with an international mall company, decided to go into his 401k and fund this event to the tune of about $50,000. Furthermore, we knew if we had to pay agencies to facilitate our advertising, public relations, social media, and all of the other necessary components needed to produce an event (which would generally cost $3,000 per month for each service), we might not get this thing off the ground. Fortunately, Andrew had extensive agency experience and had just re-launched the "UniteUs Group", which was the agency of record responsible for facilitating all of the necessary components for this initiative. Not only had I never met anyone before this point who would have the confidence and wherewithal to do something like this, I don't think I will ever meet anyone who is not independently wealthy who would put their money where their mouth is to bring their dream/vision to reality at this level. We literally created a platform to effectively highlight and showcase other people, for them to make money, at our own personal expense with no guaranteed return on investment. Andrew was aware of my financial situation at the time, and even though I lacked the financial resources to contribute, he allowed me to join him as a partner on this venture by putting in my own **"sweat equity."**

There was no road map for hosting an art fair inside of homes that people could only access via boats, but we did the best with what we had and provided an opportunity for Andrew's creative genius to come into play. We were able to get two vacant multi-million dollar homes to exhibit in that first year, and a third location on the water with a luxury residence sales center where we exhibited hundreds of thousands of dollars worth of Andrew's college professor Laurence Gartel's digital artwork from his personal collection. My dear friend Joyce, who had music label experience from her time on the West Coast, told me at the time "You just need the event to run"—and it did. The first year we didn't charge the artists to participate, had relatively inexpensive tickets for attendees, and ultimately **took a loss** which we considered an *investment in our future*, now that

Andrew was committed to seeing this vision through. And yes, somehow his recently newlywed wife stayed with him and supported us (bless her soul).

Every year we learned so much, and every year we made the experience better and better. It was a continually learning experience with the boats and the homes, the timing, how to professionally hang the art work in a way that would allow us to not damage the walls. This was on top of constantly finding new ways of connecting with realtors to encourage them to have their sellers make their multi-million dollar houses available for us to fill with art for a week, with a few days of set up and break down. We knew there was tons of value we could provide with this experience; it was a matter of showing and not just telling how we could do so. From realtors being able to provide the most glorified "luxury open house" experience imaginable for their sellers and prospective buyers, to brands being able to activate inside of properties they generally wouldn't be able to otherwise, to the countless media opportunities for the press and government to capitalize off of.

This is where my newfound partner Andrew's Swiss Army knife of skills started to become apparent. The first year we had an eight-bedroom house where they asked us "not to put holes in the walls." Needless to say, it makes things very difficult to hang artwork without putting holes in the wall, but Andrew came up with a solution to take a piece of melamine, a type of wood used to make custom closets that was tall and narrow, and gently laid it on an angle up against the wall, with soft felt stoppers on the top edge to ensure it didn't damage or scratch the lovely wallpaper. He realized we would need to secure it into the floor to prevent it from shifting, so we added a piece of Velcro tape to the bottom part to stick it to the floor. Then we made holes in the middle of these boards so the artwork could be hung in the middle of the board, making it look like it was almost hung on the wall although it wasn't. Thankfully, no one kicked or tripped on any of these boards, the fair ran with relatively minimal errors, and the feedback was overwhelmingly positive from the majority of people who attended. Of course there were some *"Debbie Downers", some "Nancy Naysayers"*, and some haters who legitimately didn't want us to succeed because they really didn't have anything better to do with their lives,but I **learned to choose** not to care and that you *couldn't please everyone.* That was a tough one, but ultimately, that one lesson helped save me a lot of stress and added years back on to my life.

You would think after the fair running the first year, followed by a successful second year (despite a few hiccups), and more and more press, that during the third year, the city/county/business community would come around. Unfortunately, despite our offer to donate portions of proceeds we weren't in a position to donate to local arts and business nonprofits who didn't need the money—they didn't come around. One of the ideas we had, which we thought was a no-brainer, involved encouraging businesses that said they "supported the arts" to close early for one day of the four-day art fair (which started on Thursday and ran until Sunday) and to bring their employees out on a boat to the fair for *team building*—but they just didn't get it. Once again, I am forever grateful for Andrew's intuition, mental strength/fortitude, and belief in our abilities to not let these setbacks discourage our efforts. We knew we were sitting on something magical, and that we didn't need validation for our efforts from a chosen few. We held some of the most memorable opening night parties in the history of Fort Lauderdale -- bringing all of the artists, sponsors, and partners involved together to celebrate with performances we'll never forget. We were continually receiving positive feedback from the artists and attendees of the fair, who told us countless times that they looked forward to this event annually more so than any other event in the community.

On a positive note, I can proudly report that we succeeded in accomplishing our initial mission statement of **"putting Fort Lauderdale on the art world map,"** as evidenced by the coverage we received in major publications like Forbes, Thrillist, Architectural Digest, PBS, NPR, and other international publications which found the concept worthwhile. This worthwhile concept ran annually for four years during the last week of January, leading the way to the creation of Fort Lauderdale Art & Design Week (FTLADW). There were so many other artists and arts organizations we would support throughout the year that we couldn't fit inside the homes, so we felt we needed to create a new/bigger platform where we could incorporate everyone who wanted to participate. This art week, similar to those in other cities across the globe, continued to grow as we weren't charging participating entities, which received the benefits of being listed in our event calendars, websites, and series of promotions. Once again, this was a form of *altruism* that Andrew and I both understood; we knew if we built it, they would come. From a marketing and public relations standpoint, this initiative, which spanned the entire county, ended up beating out over 800 other initiatives to receive multiple Public Relations Service Association (PRSA) awards, including **Best Tactics, Best Integrated Campaign, and Best of Show** for the Destination on Display. Through various reporting metrics we were able to show the reach, impact, and growth in hotel room stays on a year-over-year basis for the hotels on the beach alone, which contributed to the big driver for our county's tourism board—the bed tax which derives a small percentage from every hotel room booked (aka "heads and beds"). This made us proud, and although we haven't produced the art fair since it last took place in January 2020 right before the pandemic, we do plan to bring it back one day when we receive proper support to underwrite a six figure endeavor like this.

Highlights From Art Fort Lauderdale

- We exhibited over 500 artists & over 1000 pieces of art in 4 years of the annual art fair. Many of the artists experienced their first, and only time, exhibiting in a 4-day art fair.

- We flew in and exhibited the French collective "Obvious" for their first time participating in an art fair after their A.I.-generated artwork was the first piece to be auctioned at Christie's for $400k—a big deal at the time (2019) prior to the explosion of A.I. and NFTs.

- Led to the creation of Fort Lauderdale Art & Design Week, which paved the way for the NSU Art Museum to have artist *Rob Pruitt host his internationally recognized artistic Flea Market* at the museum during FTLADW. This is the same Flea Market concept that's taken place at The Tate, The Venice Biennale, etc.—which was and still is a big deal for establishing Fort Lauderdale as an artistic destination.

- Led in part to the creation of Zero Empty Spaces, establishing art and real estate connections that paved the way to activating 28 vacant commercial real estate spaces to create affordable working artist studios in 3 states over the last 4 years.

- Also led to the series of our "artDISCOURSE" artist talks, which ultimately led to us bringing the first African American female curator of the Brooklyn Museum (Ashley James) for a talk moderated by Bonnie Clearwater, which led to the Eric Mack connection and ultimately his solo show and various other shows at The NSU Art Museum in downtown Fort Lauderdale in addition to the Yale MFA Alumni exhibit.

- A plethora of other connections and "opportunities for creative collision" we found out about oftentimes years after the fact, including:

    - Countless people found new friends, jobs, opportunities, zest for art, romantic relationships, etc.

    - Nearly all of our partners and sponsors received immense benefit and economic impact from participating in the fair, gaining myriad new customers as a result.

- One artist who was initially skeptical and critical of the event prior to exhibiting met various valuable contacts during the fair, including ones who not only became collectors, but also invited him to fill lobbies of newly constructed condo buildings with his art.

- We had one volunteer who rediscovered herself and her artistic prowess at the fair after having attended art school earlier in life. Through the nightly after-parties we hosted during the week of the fair, this volunteer ultimately connected with a local budding arts producer and became his creative director, spawning a new career in art that led to working with an interior designer, curating art in Chicago and beyond.

- And one of the special memories personally for me was getting one of our favorite artists (Stephanie Melissa Dorsainvil) **paid** to paint a Lexus on the dock of the Pier 66 Marina as attendees of the art fair walked up to board the boats. She finished painting the wrapped vehicle at the local JM Lexus dealership which provided a great memory, experience, content, and marketing opportunity for everyone involved.

Learning lessons from ArtFTL

I wish I could tell you the journey will be filled with glitter and rainbows, but unfortunately that isn't always the case. While we all have our own unique situation in life, everyone does need to eat, and the majority of people in society generally need to work to put food on their table—unless they are independently wealthy and can do whatever they want in life. Though if you are not independently wealthy and you want to start a new venture, I have some learning lessons I want to share with you here. If something doesn't work monetarily, it doesn't matter how good of an idea it is or how much you want it to happen, **you will need to let that shit go. On every entrepreneur's journey there is a point that you need to "shit or get off of the pot," and unfortunately, some people wait too long to get off the pot.**

Have you tried a new venture? Or wanted to? How about a side hustle or passion project? Did it not go as smoothly as you would have liked it to? Did you decide, or have you not decided yet, that you might need to pivot and reevaluate your prospects?

In the midst of this journey, after putting too many miles on my car driving Uber, I had a business coach who took a liking to me and offered pro bono coaching services in exchange for promotion of his offerings. Through his coaching and evaluating my financial earning potential during my early stage entrepreneurship, he made me realize that a time was coming in which I would need to "get off of the pot" and go back to recruiting, which I did for a year and a half from late 2017 to mid 2019. It was during that time when I continued working on all of this on the side, and was able to help keep the momentum going with Andrew until I was able to rejoin "entrepreneurville" full time in May 2019 when our earning prospects were looking more promising.

While I didn't have as much invested monetarily as my partner, who opened his piggy bank to help us self fund the first year of the art fair, I have invested over four years of building something that no one can deny is a great idea. But be it the wrong place, or the wrong time, or the wrong art market, the fair unfortunately wasn't meant to be when COVID came along. This in part contributed to us postponing the fifth annual installment of the fair, which might have been the biggest blessing in disguise as our increased workload with our newest venture (Zero Empty Spaces) at that time would not have allowed us to dedicate the same time and energy we previously were able to while building something new. For those wanting to experience this "Art Fair On The Water," we are hopeful to bring the fair in the future with more partners and support. But even if we don't, it was the fair that ultimately helped me build my personal/professional credibility and image in the community, in addition to the relationships and experiences of fusing art with real estate that led to Zero Empty Spaces and subsequent successes.

If there is something you want to try and bring to life and your community, Have you tried launching a Kickstarter? Crowdfunding? Maybe a Pitch Competition? Submitting to Shark Tank? Needless to say, there are resources out there to help support your dreams and ideas - like one of our favorite groups, a goal setting/accountability/mini-mastermind we are excited to bring back called *AXEN Club*. (You can put the book down and Google it, looking up a podcast I did with the founder Dynamo, and his AAF CreativeZen talk where he shared his thought provoking and inspiring story on what led him to changing thousands of lives in the process of supporting others, and himself).

CHAPTER 8

Learning To Choose Yoga During COVID

"Yoga is the journey of the Self, Through the Self, To the Self."
- The Bhagavad Gita

While some of my business ventures took a hit during COVID, other things thrived.

Ever since I was a child, I knew I wanted to do better in life, I knew I needed to do better, and I knew I could do better. I had explored a few different personal interests with mixed success over the years, ultimately abandoning those which didn't serve the desired purpose. The majority of these explorations involved an exercise, a game, or a sport, where I would feel a sense of accomplishment upon completing the activity. The earliest of these explorations was in No Limit Texas Hold'em Poker, a game that exploded in popularity as I was exiting high school and stuck with me for 10+ years. While I had moderate success at times, the thrill of *winning* didn't surpass the disdain I had for sitting around a table with people who for the most part were miserable in life. While that game boomed in popularity, a few years later I discovered a love for a sport which was losing its popularity: racquetball. Though it makes for a lot of fun and great exercise, you ultimately need other players of similar skill level and caliber to play with. While there was a decent-sized group of people playing near where I grew up in the suburbs, racquetball players were few and far between when I moved to Fort Lauderdale in 2015, which led me to giving up the game. In the years to follow I continued exercising in the gym of my apartment building, doing cardio and lifting weights one or two days a week to stay active, but having grown up as an athlete playing lacrosse and basketball, I could tell my body wanted more.

When 2020 came around, the building I had been living in since moving to downtown Fort Lauderdale quickly became overpriced, and I was faced with yet another decision. There was a brand new building for which a friend of mine was doing public relations, and it touted a societal, community feel, filled with lots of perks, amenities, and events. It probably wasn't the best financial decision to move into Society Las Olas during a pandemic, but I knew something positive was waiting for me there and that it was time to move on from the older building that had served its purpose. When I was thinking about what was in store for me, I thought the best I could hope for was a new business contact or a potential future Mrs. Snow. But little did I know that at a time I needed it more than ever, my life would change in the way I needed it the most. I rediscovered my zest for learning and growing in a whole new way.

It was on my second trip to Tulum, Mexico with my nonprofit The Ocean Rescue Alliance when the shift happened, and only now that I have some appreciation for portals and vortexes can I recognize this shift. The second day we were there, we arose early to see the sunrise, and headed to the north end of the beach in the state park where the lighthouse was located, south of the Tulum ruins. I was developing a hobby of making videos for social media to document my adventures, flying my newly acquired drone and doing time lapses of sunrises with my GoPro to show my friends and family. This was at a time when I didn't necessarily need more hobbies, but felt it could be beneficial to our business ventures and initiatives for me to have these skills/resources. Little did I know that after I used up all of my batteries that morning capturing the sunrise, I would discover a hobby that was way more beneficial to my life than anything I could have ever imagined or experienced before.

My nonprofit partner decided to start trekking up the beach to explore the ruins of a vacant lighthouse we were supporting the restoration of, approximately a ten-minute walk each way, which left her friend who was with us on this trip and myself with some time waiting around on the beach. And then, it happened. Her friend, whom I had only just met the day before, somehow had the intuition to turn and say to me, **"Hey, do you want to do some yoga?"** To which I responded, "sure". It was at this moment that the "*portal*" opened up for me, and life would never be the same again. This friend was not a trained yoga instructor, just a practitioner, and he had discovered the practice was beneficial for his life in his early twenties. It started off innocently enough, as I began following along while he moved into some standard yoga poses including planks, sun salutations, and downward dogs (otherwise known as a *vinyasa flow*). I thought to myself, "Well, this isn't as difficult as I remember it," recollecting the one time I tried to "flow" on the beach previously with an old high school classmate who was going through her certification, though the practice at that time didn't resonate with me.

We probably practiced for ten or fifteen minutes, but inevitably as I would come to find out, that was all I needed. I remember we were on the go a lot on that trip and weren't going to have time for cardio or working out aside from walking up and down the beach, but almost instantly I began feeling **better** after this little practice. I was taking my health more seriously after getting diagnosed with type 1 diabetes earlier in the year just after the beginning of the pandemic, and would do cardio a few times a week but not as much as I could have or should have. I always stretched beforehand, remembering calisthenics from warming up in my lacrosse days, but those light stretches were not like this and were not done with the same intention. A lot of people said at the beginning of the pandemic that they wanted to come out of it better than they went into it, and I also shared similar sentiments but was missing the catalyst for change. I had bought some exercise bands for home workouts in my apartment, would ride my bike a little farther than I previously had to get fresh air, but was not honestly pushing myself to that next level to realize the changes my body desperately needed and was secretly yearning for.

Fortunately, by November 2020 I had moved into this new building where an old mutual acquaintance from the arts district, Chloe Ravel, was leading a free yoga class in the mornings, located on my new beautiful twenty-fifth floor open space area overlooking most of Broward County. A few weeks after moving in and prior to the Tulum trip, I had gone up to this space one morning to marvel at the sunrise, flying my drone during the yoga class which Chloe kindly invited me to join, though I had no real intention of pursuing yoga at that time. Well, that all changed after I connected with a young, attractive woman living in the building, who I saw via her Instagram was going to this 7:30 A.M. yoga class. While passing the time in Tulum I asked Chloe via Instagram DM if she would "put in a good word for me" with this girl, which prompted her to reply with the words that would change my life: "come to yoga." Needless to say, that was the invitation I needed, and to spare the details I don't care to recount, the girl inevitably disappeared but the yoga, meditation, mindfulness, and all of the other benefits remain in my life.

It was the feeling of my body opening up for me initially, in ways I had never felt before, that did it for me and really started me on this journey. For anyone who's ever done an hour-long yoga class, you'll never forget that first "**savasana**" ("*corpse pose*"), where you lie on your back after finishing the physical *flow* portion of the class and have an opportunity to just be there with your thoughts, feeling amazing. Then I found out there was more to yoga, including breathing, meditation, sound bowls, and this little thing I had been missing out on called "**mindfulness**" that became prevalent in my life as a major game changer. I was constantly on the go before COVID, doing my best to balance all of my community projects/initiatives, and had already burnt myself out multiple times over in the first few years of my entrepreneurial journey. Despite not taking my exercising habits as seriously as I could have the first six months of the pandemic, I was now a man on a mission. I started with the one morning class offered per week religiously, then discovered there was a second free class another night during the week that was even more of a *chill vinyasa flow* (a method of yoga in which movements form a flowing sequence in coordination with the breath). I was hooked.

Then I discovered **Yoga With Adriene on YouTube** and the immense amount of resources available on the internet for free if you searched for them. As a result, I developed a daily practice of much-needed movement. While it didn't always include a full **flow** it was essential in helping me stay grounded and balanced, as well as making my body change in ways I had always dreamt of. I was starting to see my abs from all of the planks, my shoulders stopped shaking while in the *downward dog pose* and became well defined, and I was starting to feel openings in different parts of my body I would later find out were related to our chakras (energy centers). Fast forward six months to me becoming Chloe's most regular and loyal student in the building, I made another decision I always wanted to but had hesitated making: I engaged Chloe for her paid coaching program. While this initially was to help take my yoga practice to the next level, the introduction of new healing modalities, mindfulness practices, and energy work took not only my yoga practice to the next level but my whole life. This included one-on-one **sound bowl healing sessions, Reiki, Theta Healing**, and so much more. The implementation of my new daily morning routine that we developed and began expanding upon helped me start my day with more clarity than Adderall or Vyvanse ever could. This included waking up to positive affirmations, then listening to motivational speakers' videos on YouTube while eating my breakfast, followed by morning meditation, and finally capped off by at a minimum some yoga stretches if I didn't have time for a full flow. My mornings, my days, and my life have never been the same since. The level of energy, alertness, and care for the communities I serve and the work that I do reached new heights, higher than I could have ever hoped for *naturally*. The level of connection I've been able to establish with my friends, family, and even strangers has been incredible. For all of the times I would say "everything happens for a reason," this one definitely did and I am forever grateful for the impact Chloe Ravel had on my life, the work we did together, and for her being there for me as a friend/guide/guru.

Chloe was there for me in ways I could never fully describe in this book or many others, at a time when I needed her the most. Unfortunately, while this next part isn't fun or easy to remember - I felt it was important to vulnerably share. The woman in my building I had pursued to get into yoga ultimately led me on in conversation over a period of time, expressing interest in conversations to the point that I assumed and hoped she would give me a chance romantically. On paper, she seemed like a great catch, but on some level I knew something was off about her intentions. She had opened up to me when it was pretty apparent she wasn't opening up to other people in the building (at least at yoga), and I thought admiring from afar, starting off as friends, and eventually building a close connection could show her I was a good potential partner, similar to how I thought she was a good match for me. After a few months, it appeared her interest came around more as we began going out and spending more time together. But the way the story goes is—it wasn't meant to be, and the best thing that didn't happen to me was probably the best thing to happen for me.

Out of the blue one day, this woman *ghosted* me, stopping all communication. This sudden halt in our friendship/communication was hard for me, and it got worse when I ran into her in our apartment building's elevator after weeks of not talking - with someone who ended up becoming her new boyfriend. To make things more complicated for me internally, a series of strange coincidences, run-ins, and interactions took place around this time with this woman, and the signals before the elevator run-in were more than mixed. I was starting to experience deep emotional trauma, anxiety, and at times depression, having thought I was on the path to my first promising romantic relationship in years. In my mind this would have made for a great story, since she was the one I attributed with getting me into yoga and inspiring a change in my life for the better. I continually beat myself up over this story way too hard, and thankfully, my coach and friend Chloe was there to have my back and save me a ton more misery.

She knew which mindful exercise, breathing technique, and healing modality I should apply as I kept her abreast of this situation which was weighing heavily on me. More so than that, around this time Chloe introduced me to the work of Dr. Joe Dispenza, a man who changed my life and many others. Dr. Joe's postgraduate training includes the fields of neuroscience and neuroplasticity, quantitative electroencephalogram (QEEG) measurements, epigenetics, mind-body medicine, and brain/heart coherence. Suffice it to say, he is on the cutting edge of helping people heal themselves through the power of the mind, as outlined in his most notable book, *Breaking the Habit of Being Yourself*. It was this book, and some of the key lessons and takeaways which Chloe helped reiterate into my brain, that helped me get through this dark and difficult time of disappointment and despair. At this time I found living in Fort Lauderdale no longer served me, and I didn't want to have any more chance encounters with the aforementioned woman in my building or around town, so it was time for a change in scenery.

I inevitably moved out of this building after my first-year lease, and while not having access to two free yoga classes via an elevator ride weekly was disappointing at first, it actually served as a blessing in disguise. Fortunately, the building I subsequently moved into in downtown Hollywood with my new roommate (Seth, aka The Mindful Doctor, who was also a certified yoga instructor and dedicated practitioner) had a yoga studio literally one block away on the same street. This is where I would develop my **studio practice**, and fall even deeper in love with yoga. The schedule of offerings was phenomenal, and for $100 per month I could take as many classes as I wanted, which would occasionally peak at twenty-five per month. While taking classes with an infrared heater helped me push my mind, body, and soul further than I ever had before, there was a whole other realm of yoga I was about to discover. Thankfully, at this studio these weren't all traditional vinyasa (active) classes that you might think of, but almost more important to me was the introduction of **yin yoga**—a much slower, grounded, restorative flow which included holding your body in passive positions for 2-5 minutes each. This allowed for opening of new space in my back, shoulders, hips, and parts of my body I did not know existed. Most times these were in the evening, after long days of work, and I had never experienced a better way to unwind than lying on my yoga mat, as an adult, and giving my body the time and space it needed to recover.

The teachers were amazing, coming from all different backgrounds and walks of life, and I truly felt at home with my newfound tribe and newfound vibe. Simultaneously, I had continued diving deeper into my personal development journey and seeing how much growth I could accomplish. While my weekly sessions with Chloe ended after our three-month coaching program concluded, we continued working together monthly and she thankfully was there for me to help take my yoga practice to even greater heights, while instructing me on ways to maneuver my body to avoid injury, which is key. Through this exploration and development of my studio practice I met so many new friends, experienced so much growth mentally and physically, and fortunately was there to support my new roommate and friend Seth in a pet project he wanted to start that he described to me as a "Conscious Men's Circle," which would meet weekly. While I loved interpersonal communication, personal development, and in-person meetings, if you would have told me I would be involved in a men's group just a year before this, I don't know what I would have said. Fortunately, with two other like-minded men we knew, we formed our local chapter of the Arka Brotherhood and began holding weekly meetings in our apartment. While we don't practice yoga in the meetings, there are many mindful components, including opening each meeting with three rounds of **Wim Hof breathing**, shares of gratitude, and other mindful exercise intended to help us connect to ourselves and each other on a deeper level. At the time of writing this, I've been attending our weekly circle for one year now, and don't know where I would be without it. These meetings serve as a therapeutic healing session for me and my fellow brothers more so than anything else. It's not really that spiritual or "woo-woo," but it definitely takes an open mind and some conscious intention to do this work, and I could never thank the practice of yoga enough for opening me up to this world I did not know existed. There are very few things that I cannot endorse more than considering starting your own yoga practice. It might just change your life.

Learning Lesson

Have you thought about taking your life to the next level? Is there some self-improvement work you've wanted to do but have been putting off trying? Have you tried something a second time after it might not have worked out as perfectly as it could have the first time? What is self-care to you? I encourage you to put the book down and take a deep moment of reflection on these questions. After you do so, pick up a journal, a Post-it Note, or voice recorder and relay the thoughts that flow through your mind onto whichever method you choose to permanently put them into the universe. Revisit them, maybe in a week or maybe in a month, and look back on how far you've grown since you initially answered those questions. The sky truly is the limit, and I hope to see you on the mountaintop one day.

Chapter 9

Learning To Choose Not Giving Up

"Everyone you know is fighting a battle you know nothing about, friendly reminder to be kind - always." - **Socrates (paraphrased)**

Let me tell you something: It would have been a lot easier to give up—so many times. Sitting here writing this from 2021-2023, I can't believe I've gotten this far when it would have been so much easier to give up on countless occasions. But I think to myself, where would that have gotten me? Back to square one? Sitting at a desk as a recruiter wondering what if?

One of the most basic, tried-and-true methods I've followed for staying motivated and focused with my eyes on the prize has been listening to motivational talks on YouTube daily. As part of the morning routine I've adopted over the last two years, I've followed my affirmation rituals (which start immediately upon waking up) with a steady rotation of endless motivational talks on various YouTube playlists comprised from the likes of David Goggins, Jim Rohn, Les Brown, Jordan Peterson, Kobe Bryant, Joe Rogan, Gary Vee, Tony Robbins, Jocko Willink, Joe Dispenza, Alan Watts, and the other phenomenal speakers these YouTube channels choose to incorporate. As I previously alluded to, I've always been a fan of talks from my early YouTube/ TEDTalk days, but could never have imagined the impact they would have until we got to the COVID times. A few weeks into the pandemic, I was told a guy I went to high school with—a successful attorney with an attractive girlfriend and seemingly all of the things in the world going for him—killed himself. A few months after that, as we were all going through tough times in an uncertain world, I had dinner and drinks one day and lunch the following day with two dear friends of mine whom I appreciated/respected deeply. I assumed both of them were doing well, all things considered, and I admired both of them for their growth and progress in their respective fields/journeys.

Then both of them told me, within a few hours of one another, that they were contemplating **suicide**, or what life would be like *if they were not here*. To say I truly was not prepared for that would be an understatement, but I'm forever grateful I was there and present to have received that information and was there to support them that day and the days that followed. While thankfully they did not take their own lives, this series of events left an indelible impression on my life. Fortunately for my friends, family, and myself, I had not ever realistically considered suicide. Seemingly, on paper and in actuality, I have had so much going for me, from early on when teachers and guidance counselors would tell my parents, "Evan has all the potential in the world," to when I finally actualized that potential in my thirties after partnering with Andrew and starting our various initiatives. I have since gone on to form relationships and befriend thousands of artists, exhibiting hundreds of them through our various platforms, as well as to become a respected member of the community and art world whom people told me they appreciate. But now the thought began to creep up in the back of my mind: *Would anyone miss me if I were gone?* Does anyone really care about the **work** we're doing and all of our struggles when very few show up to our rescue or even to support us? What would the scene in my native home community of Broward County look like if we weren't there anymore, cheering on the arts with our pom-poms and trying to get people to keep caring?

"You can only control the things you can control" is a saying I've had in my mind for years and would continually reiterate to people. This is your life, your business, your situation, and what happens, the bad and the good, is all you can control. Maybe I needed to write this book and put pen to paper to really have this hit home for me. I am not perfect, I struggle with imposter syndrome, I struggle with "what if" syndrome, and I used to struggle with crying about things being unfair or not going our way. The bitterness and jadedness used to come out a lot more often, and a lot more freely; those around me at that time would hear me question out loud, "Why doesn't the business community support us? Why isn't the government supporting us? Why aren't the grant makers supporting us?" Looking back on it, and thankfully better understanding it now with my mindfulness perspective, I wasted a lot of time, and I mean a **lot of time**, on things I couldn't control. But at some point after this wakeup call in life, at some point during COVID (around the time I got into mindfulness and meditation), I started caring less about how unfair these situations were and what everyone else thought, and more about providing for myself and my family. We built our brands on altruism, and I built my personal reputation on being genuine—and I always will. But the aforementioned groups that haven't supported us like they do our contemporaries, they don't care if I eat or go starving. I care if I eat or not, and that is something I can control. I've wanted to double down on Zero Empty Spaces and our out-of-state expansion plans, as it is our first business actually generating real revenue that can afford me the way of life I've worked for, and in all reality deserve. But I also made verbal, long term commitments to the community which, despite the fact that I'm not a politician or city commissioner, I want to keep as part of my mission and legacy to be the **"greatest human being in Broward County history."** Even though I have already done more than 99% of private citizens in Broward County history have done to actualize that goal, that might not ever be the case. I might not ever get a plaque, or a trophy, or a street named after me. People very well might forget all of the wonderful things we did for years, with our own money, that we didn't have to do. But I sleep very well at night knowing I did what I could, with what I had, because I can only control the things I can control—and not giving up was one of them.

I'm sure I'll be asked about the 1000 Mermaids Artificial Reef Project and Ocean Rescue Alliance International non-profits I co-founded and sit on the board of, which I purposefully chose to save stories of for a future book. While the intention is pure, and the potential for the impact that is needed to save our oceans/reefs is immense, small minded people and their shallow egos made me want to give up on this project time and time again. If I told you all of the ways how various members of the science community, academic community, and government employees got in the way of us doing a good thing by deploying these artistically crafted artificial reefs at a time when our oceans need them the most – we would have another book on our hands. But one of the things that my partner on this endeavor (Shelby Thomas, the next Jane Goodall/Sylvia Earle for the oceans) continually reminds me of, is that I'm glad we **both didn't give up** in spite of the unnecessary roadblocks that were continually put in our way. These reefs provide so much joy to so many people, in addition to the environmental and economic benefits they provide to the areas where we deploy them – that giving up on this project would be doing a disservice to the planet. So needless to say, I'm glad I didn't give up, which prompts me to insert a few of my favorite David Goggins quotes here from his best selling book "**Can't Hurt Me: Master Your Mind and Defy the Odds**":

- "The most important conversations you'll ever have are the ones you'll have with yourself."

- "Everything in life is a mind game! Whenever we get swept under by life's dramas, large and small, we are forgetting that no matter how bad the pain gets, no matter how harrowing the torture, all bad things end."

- "Only you can master your mind, which is what it takes to live a bold life filled with accomplishments most people consider beyond their capability."

- "If you want to be one of the few to defy those trends in our ever-softening society, you will have to be willing to go to war with yourself and create a whole new identity, which requires an open mind."

- "Denial is the ultimate comfort zone."

Learning Lesson - To never give up

Was there a time you wanted to give up? Aren't you glad you didn't? I know you persevered or you wouldn't be reading this right now. :) Are there people who look up to you? Who admire you? Who love you? Can you imagine what life would be like if they found out you gave up, when as little as a few words and a few pieces of positive affirmations could have made a difference in your life and the lives of those around you? What things have you heard of, learned, or experienced which you could implement into your life? Have you ever listened to the "Motiversity" channel on YouTube? It might not be anything special, but if this resonates with you at all I encourage you to **tune in** to the free messages, movements, and motivations out there. This might just be the impetus you need to persist and to take your life to the next level.

CHAPTER 10

Learning To Choose Helping Others

"It's really important & really meaningful that we are cultivating some sort of Creative Community in Fort Lauderdale. I really wanna thank you guys for showing up to other people's stuff. I really want to encourage you to show up to other people's stuff because that's how we're going to grow the Creative Community."

- Tim Hasse

I guess you could say I was brought into this world to live a life of service. My parents, G-d Bless them, love helping people. They met through Landmark Education back in the day, in Werner Erhard's EST training, part of the advanced course track past the weekend long **Landmark Forum** that, to a certain extent, predates similar modern events like Gratitude Training and Tony Robbins. My parents' love for these platforms, and service, was instilled in me from a young age, as they had me take the Landmark Forum for children in Washington D.C. when I was in the fifth grade. All I can really recall now from that early experience was "not to run a racket," referring to letting "stinking thinking" and negative talk/thought patterns resonate in your mind. I guess that kind of predated some of the work I love from Dr. Joe Dispenza in *Breaking The Habit Of Being*

Yourself and all of his other phenomenal work. Nevertheless, be it from my father helping advocate to bring the game of lacrosse to prominence and inevitably the FHSAA public school system in the state of Florida (earning him an inaugural spot in the Florida Chapter of the US Lacrosse Hall Of Fame) or my mother's countless sponsees she supported through her work in the recovery space between AA/AL-anon/CODA/etc and other groups, I learned to love the process of genuinely helping people because it's the right thing to do—altruistically.

So I guess it was my destiny that I was called into this life of service, first by entering the world of recruiting and **helping people** get placed into their future roles, which led to my path of self discovery, TED talks, Gary Vee, and eventually entrepreneurville. When I was first getting started with Choose954, I merely wanted to "show the people I grew up with in Coral Springs all of the cool things that were going on in FATvillage/FTL so it could give them a reason to Choose the 954 and come back" at a macro level. When I started getting more granular and in deep with the artists I was forming relationships with in the arts districts, I truly just wanted to show people—with my cell phone and Facebook live initially—that there was cool stuff going on in OUR community (which at the time the majority of people did not know about). The wins might have been so small back then, but I cherished and celebrated **each and every single one of them**. I vividly remember leaving events, meetings, and coffee shops with my cup so full it was overflowing with positive energy and emotions. If you were a part of one of those – Thank You.

I wish more people would tell me about their wins to which I've helped contribute to over the years, not because I need a payback or credit, but because that shit is my **oxygen** and puts air in my lungs. That is the shit that keeps me going, when an artist tells me, "Thank you, because I did this thing you suggested I do (or did with you), I just sold $10,000+ worth of artwork to one collector." That might not seem like a lot, or that might seem like $1,000,000 to you, but hearing those stories and feedback is what motivates me to keep going and keep impacting others. If we did all this good, and no one cared, no one provided feedback, no one complained, and we were just in a vacuum—there is no oxygen.

I could write a book on all of the moments I remember and all of the moments I've forgotten when we changed people's lives, but I'll include only a few of the more recent ones which I feel are worth mentioning here. As I began getting more involved in my new community of Hollywood, Florida in 2022, I connected with the curator of our city's art and culture center, as well as our community redevelopment agency's arts coordinator, to establish a new component of our annual Fort Lauderdale Art &

Design Week with the creation of an "Art Hollywood" weekend. The goal was to create a day for open studios to highlight and showcase all of the talented artists working and residing in the great city of Hollywood, which unfortunately oftentimes is in the shadows of Miami and the stepchild to Fort Lauderdale or even Palm Beach, to a certain extent.

When the event finally came to fruition with dozens of artists participating, I went around that day with a photo and video crew to document the artists working in their studios, the tours taking place, and the pop-up activations as part of this new event to storytell and showcase for marketing purposes. While I was doing so, something became apparent to me that maybe I took for granted, or never really stopped to think about: Some artists never have people tour their studios, let alone have a photographer and videographer come in to produce high quality recaps.

Without naming anyone in particular, there's something I want to share regarding a few conversations I had with artists that day who are noteworthy and established in their own regard, and who call Hollywood home. Hollywood is admittedly a little bit of a funny place, having once been an old sleepy beach town that has since come a long way to cement itself as one of the top cities to live in Broward County and South Florida, with a bevy of things to do and explore throughout the city's limits. One of the artists I had a deeper conversation with that day was an older

Hollywood native who had moved to Boston after high school and established a very successful art career spanning decades, having written books and completed numerous noteworthy nonprofit projects. This artist was preparing to return to Hollywood in the weeks leading up to the event we were putting together, and after being connected to us to participate and receive some marketing support, he shared how he was so moved to see all of the progress that had been made in his hometown. He transparently shared his initial hesitation in coming back to a place that was previously referred to as a "cultural wasteland," having come from a well cultured city like Boston, and was grateful that Andrew and I had taken the amount of time out of our lives that we had to promote and support the arts. That conversation, his genuine gratitude, and the books, t-shirts, and merch he gave me to say thanks really stuck with me – cementing the feeling that the event was a **success** even if it didn't attract *thousands of attendees.*

I guess this is a great time to plug in one of my favorite quotes: *"Turnout is not indicative of success."* Sometimes success is a smile, a hug, a high five, or just people "showing up to other people's stuff" (another one of my favorite sayings). The other story from that day I feel is worth mentioning came from conversation, smiles, and feedback I had from another established artist who had actually recently been featured on a Netflix show based around their respective creative medium. This conversation happened after a demo they hosted in their studio, which is located in the Hollywood Arts Park in the heart of downtown Hollywood—one of the city's hubs for community events and gatherings. Despite having established their creative practice to the point they have multiple similar studios on cruise ships as an activation, being a fan favorite for date night activities, and having their artwork being well collected, the artist shared with me that they didn't always feel "the love" from their community to the extent that they could have. I understood that feeling, which paved the way for some of the most thought provoking, inspiring, and comforting conversation I ever had with an artist I admired. Through this conversation, they felt encouraged that the needle was moving forward in the right direction as a result of the new initiatives taking place, and their feeling of new hope left me feeling proud that I could connect a few dots to provide a positive spark in the life of someone whom I admire and respect. Wins come in all shapes and sizes; they don't always have a price tag associated with them, and don't always translate to a "return on investment" (ROI) in the near or long-term future. Unfortunately, a lot of people get hung up on the transactional nature of our capitalistic society, thinking that there always has to be a "give/get"—but fortunately, my business partner helped me multiply the altruism genes hidden inside my DNA. With a little help from Gary Vaynerchuk's talks encouraging like-minded entrepreneurs to "play the long game," I remain hopeful with a positive outlook that the future ahead of us is bright. Another favorite saying of mine from Gary is "1 > 0" – something he preached by articulating that he rather have one person's life be impacted by his efforts than thousands of people participating who truly won't receive the impact. It took a while for me to process that initially, but once it sat in, it has become one of my guiding principles and favorite reminders.

These are just a few short stories that come to mind, providing an opportunity for me to share that **this** is why I do what I do – because you never know how you simply *caring* can make a difference in someone's life, whether they are established or not.

Learning Lesson

Have you ever done a random act of kindness? Mentored someone you had the ability to support? Joined a mini mastermind group like AXEN Club to help support random peers with your goals? Help is out there and available, and help is on the way—if you're present and show up for it. I encourage you to give someone in whom you see potential a piece of positive feedback, solicited or not, because you never know how that spark could light a fire inside of them to change their life, their community, or even change the world.

CHAPTER 11

Learning To Choose Men's Work And Self-Care

"Don't stop when you're tired, stop when you're done. Stay hard!"
- **David Goggins** (If you've never heard of him, go buy his book "Can't Hurt Me" and thank me later!)

As I was grooving through life on my personal development journey, I was elated when I discovered **yoga** and all of the rabbit holes you can go down with the various *branches, teachings, and lessons.* Developing a yoga practice, following the yogi lifestyle, and receiving all of the benefits of the practice has had a profound impact on my life, helping to reshape my thought processes and my worldview. This new lens, new outlook, and new lifestyle would have been more than enough for me as part of my journey to living my best/most optimal life – but fortunately, I was destined to find an invitation to discover even more to see how deep this rabbit hole goes. About a year after I began my yoga practice, I was invited to a mini mastermind group meetup for "light workers" by a friend of mine who shares a zest for optimizing her life and continual growth and development. Most of the attendees were similarly also on their journey into meditation and mindfulness, and reading books by the likes of Dr. Joe Dispenza (a personal favorite of mine). However, one of the attendees, who was also invited by a mutual friend of ours (thanks Raw Chef Carla), stuck out as someone I was instantly connected to and comfortable talking with. While we had not met in person before, I had seen him on Instagram under his "Mindful Doctor" profile as a holistic dentist who also appeared to be into yoga, mindfulness, optimizing a healthy lifestyle, and personal development. After the meeting, we struck up a conversation and realized we had a lot more in common than we could have discovered on our respective Instagram pages. At this time, I had recently made the decision to move out of downtown Fort Lauderdale as it was being overdeveloped and too expensive, and was beginning my search for places in one of the surrounding cities in Broward County where I call home. When I mentioned this to my newfound friend Seth, aka The Mindful Doctor, he mentioned he too was looking for a new place to live, and we discussed getting together for dinner and yoga to get to know one another better and explore the possibilities. Fortunately for me, I guess I was in the right place at the right time with the right mindset, as this chance interaction and connection prompted me to learn about a new outlet in life I've since integrated and have become grateful for.

I should start off by saying that Seth possesses one of the most incredible wealths of knowledge on the human body and how to optimize it to live a healthy and balanced life. More so than that, his generosity and altruistic nature of genuinely wanting to share this knowledge he's acquired with his fellow humans and the community at large through his social media channel and **podcast ("Art Of Mindful Medicine")** is unlike that of anyone else I've had the fortune to know personally. But getting to know Seth at such a pivotal time in my life as my yoga practice was developing into a studio practice down the street from our new building had me learn to consider new things. I knew there were going to be benefits of the "social experiment" of sorts by having the opportunity to live with a doctor, let alone the **mindful doctor**, but the ability to casually turn to someone you look up to and say, "I have a question for the mindful doctor," and get raw, genuine, and unfiltered feedback has been paramount in my growth process. For this alone, I am forever grateful for him, but serendipitously we were destined for more—and I had no idea how much more I was in store for.

A few weeks after we moved into a new building in downtown Hollywood together, Seth shared that he was involved with something that was new to me: a "conscious men's group" that met weekly online. I remember it being described to me as a safe space, a container of sorts, for men to get together to share their thoughts, feelings, and hold each other accountable. Well, that sounded pretty good if you asked me, and I became intrigued.

This was being done online via Zoom, thanks in part to the Zoom era we lived in during the pandemic, but Seth expressed his desire to start a group like this in person. Never being one to deter others from pursuing their dreams or ideas, I started taking more of an interest in what Seth shared regarding this group, and became open to supporting his vision of starting it in person merely by joining and showing up to participate. Fortunately, Seth was able to connect with another man who similarly was doing *the work* virtually with an online group, and had also nurtured his love of this type of work. They began speaking and meeting, and just a few months later we had an in-person conscious men's circle group meeting weekly on Wednesdays in our place from 6:30-9:30 pm.

The format was structured though also loose and free flowing, but the intent and direction was there. We would come together, start the meetings with a few rounds of **Wim Hof Breathing** to get us into an optimal mind state, share a round of gratitude, and then go into a round of weekly three-minute check-ins, recounting how our previous week had gone and highlighting the thoughts, feelings, and emotions that were present with it. After the round was complete, we would dive deeper into what was pressing for a certain member of the group that week, and give them time, space, and support to share what was on their mind. This, ***this*** in fact is where the magic started happening.

We started with five members, all of us coming from different walks of life, backgrounds, socio-economic statuses, but with the same common goal and mission: to hold space for one another in a loving and compassionate way despite not being family. This is where I achieved internal growth I was yearning for that had yet to be explored in my first thirty-six years of life.

Sure I have friends, family, confidants, and my business partner with whom I can share things. But stepping into these meetings, and being comfortable in this container, allowed me to not only open up and share crucial thought processes in my life, but allowed me to be there reciprocally for these other men who quickly became brothers and friends. After the check-ins and extended sharing times, we would steer the conversations in certain directions, sometimes with a specific prompt or exercise that would cause us to reflectively think on pertinent parts of our lives. Some of these exercises that come to mind and stick out more than others are "father shares" and "mother shares," where we were given an allotted period of time to share with the group our thoughts, memories, experiences, and learning lessons from our parents. Digging up old memories from our childhood was beneficial, though hearing my fellow brothers sharing their experiences with family and how it shaped them into the men they became certainly helped put things in context for me.

There are various levels to the exercises, meetings, and practices of doing men's work, or any group work. Sometimes you go into the meeting energized, and one week you may be tired. Some weeks you might have a lot going on in your life that's very heavy, some weeks you might not have much to share and get to sit back as a conscious observer/supporter. Some weeks you might feel more prone to give support and feedback to the person sharing in the group; some weeks you might need more feedback than you could have recognized or acknowledged. Through these free-flowing conversations and journeys, we get to know one another, what fuels us, and what grinds our gears. These exercises are the types I love, being a sucker for in-person face-to-face human interaction and connection; they truly do fuel my soul. It's easy to get off track in life, but it's easier to stay on track when you have men who show up for one another every week, week after week, and want to see each other succeed and do their best in life with their respective situation.

We don't like to consider it therapy as none of us are therapists, though we find this work to be very therapeutic. Having not seen a psychiatrist since I was a child, these exercises in humanity have helped me open up in ways that years of therapy might not have been able to accomplish. One of the most profound and simplest breakthroughs I've found in the first few months of the circle is the ability to tell another man that you **love them**. Up until this point in life, I don't think I really told another man, aside from my immediate family and possibly my business partner, that I love him. The thought, intention, and emotion behind those words have helped me reshape how I view relationships and the energy and intention I put into the interactions I have with those I choose to share my time and energy with. It's that level of consciousness, that thought and consideration, that has become one of the most impactful parts of my **self-care routine**. Up there with my daily affirmations, meditation, yoga, sauna, yoga nidra (NSDR), gratitude, and relaxing components of my day, the continual evolution and development of the group is something that fuels my soul along with my fellow brothers on this journey. Be it book recommendations, vitamins and supplements, stretches, breathing techniques, different plant based medicines, or types of water and tea, we're continually learning, growing, and evolving together. At the time of writing this book, we've been undergoing these meetings weekly for the last 11 months, and plan to continue indefinitely for hopefully the rest of our lives. Just recently, we rented an AirBnB on the other side of the state in Naples Florida and went on our first *weekend retreat* to disconnect, unwind, and go even deeper. The exercises on this venture were truly some of the most impactful I've ever participated in, between holotropic breathing, diving into masculine archetypes, thoughtful journaling, and the group favorite – "king's chair," where we broke through to even deeper levels of trust, connection, and brotherhood.

One of the most powerful exercises of my lifetime, the "king's chair" gave each one of us an opportunity to sit in front of the collective group in a semi-circle setup. We started by having the person sitting in the king's chair say, "I am a king because _____" for three minutes, stating their thoughts, qualifications, and justifications as to why they are a "king" of their own castle of sorts. The group listened and took those thoughts into consideration, and then once that round was over we transitioned to the intense part of the exercise by having the group take five minutes to communicate in a rapid fire format their thoughts on our brother's lifestyle by stating, "You are not a king because _____." Some of the feedback landed soft and almost joking in nature, but some of the feedback and thoughts we were sharing struck us deeply and presented some much needed thought provoking reflection. As the exercise started, I initially dreaded my turn to hear what my brothers were going to say about me, but knew it was necessary. This was made possible only by the trust I had within the group, through the months of work we had done up until this point sharing vulnerably and transparently. While we sat in the king's chair receiving the feedback we were to remain silent, merely nodding, smirking, eye gazing, and acknowledging the insights we were receiving. The next round of the exercise was much less dreadful, where the group had the same opportunity to rapid fire their thoughts on the opposite side of the coin, stating, "You are a king because_____." This feedback left a few of us with tears in our eyes, and truly brought us all closer together almost instantaneously. After that round was over, the man in the king's chair had an opportunity to share his thoughts on the feedback he had received, and I truly feel our lives all changed for the better in those chairs at that moment. The rest of the weekend was one of the most memorable trips I've ever had, preparing meals and cleaning up together, sharing thoughtful food with sustainably sourced ingredients Seth picked up from the farm. If I never do anything else in my life for my own personal development, I can truly consider this the mountaintop – and I am forever grateful I was in the right place at the right time to have this opportunity afforded to me by my friend and now my brother, Dr. Seth Gilson.

Learning Lesson

Do you love human interaction and connection? Ever tried a meetup? Or a mini mastermind group? Don't know where to find one in your community? Have you looked on meetup.com? Or weeklymensgroup.com? There are people, resources, and communities available everywhere in the world, although these might not manifest in your life the same way they manifested for me. Maybe these people are waiting to be found in your yoga community? Or at monthly breakfast lecture series like CreativeZen? Or on the interwebs? If you're seeking something better for yourself, your life, your community, and the world, maybe you can step outside of your comfort zone and find it. It might take some dedication, a few hours out of your life per week/month/year, but I can nearly guarantee that if you show up, and are present, it will be worth it.

I'd love to hear what you thought of the book and provide any insight I can to help. I just ask that you provide a review on Amazon if you can because they tell me that helps the algorithm and all of those things, so I can have a wider reach and make a bigger impact through this story. I truly appreciate you reading this far, and provided some additional value after this with some recommendations from things I previously alluded to and valuable parts of my life, self care routine, and daily practices.

Additionally, if you would like to work with me 1-On-1, I am beginning to make Coaching Offerings available. You can find out more and schedule by visiting -https://calendly.com/evansnow-learning-to-choose

I found having a friend, coach, and book writing accountability partner beneficial as some of the various forms of support I needed to help bring this dream to reality. I want to give a big thank you to my friend Ernesto Mandowsky for supporting me in putting pen to paper by holding me accountable, motivating me, and sitting down for our book writing sessions over the last two years.

And of course, if you ever have any questions, drop me an e-mail to evan@learningtochoose.com

Some Recommendations To Help Improve Your Life Even More

My Morning Routine (Which You Can Modify To Work For You)

- Wake Up, Immediately Have A Moment Of Gratitude For Whatever Comes To Mind

- Followed By Immediately Turning On A Different Affirmation Video On YouTube Daily (Find A Channel That Works For You)

- Followed By A Brief 5 Minute Mobility Routine In And Getting Out Of Bed. (Once Again, Find One That Works For You)

- Followed By Listening To Motivational Talks On YouTube While Eating Breakfast And Taking Vitamins/Supplements (From Various Channels)

- Followed By Morning Meditation Practice (I Aim For Atleast 5-10 Minutes Of Guided Meditation, Do Whatever Works For You)

- Followed By Morning Yoga Flow Or Stretch (10-15 Minutes, Do What Works For You)

- Followed By Cold Shower

- If You Have Access To A Sauna, Highly Recommend Incorporating Into Routine

Podcast Recommendations:

- The Joe Rogan Experience
- Huberman Lab Podcast - By Dr. Andrew Huberman
- Art Of Mindful Medicine - By Dr. Seth Gilson

Book Recommendations:

- "Start With Why" - Simon Sinek
- "Breaking The Habit Of Being Yourself" - Dr. Joe Dispenza
- "The Yamas And Niyamas" - Deborah Adele
- "Can't Hurt Me" & "Never Finished" - David Goggins
- "Living With A SEAL" - Jesse Itzler (About Having David Goggins Come Live With Him)
- "How To Change Your Mind" - Michael Pollen
- "The Four Agreements" & "The Fifth Agreement" - don Miguel Ruiz
- "Outliers" - Malcolm Gladwell
- "Be Here Now" - Ram Dass

- "The Immortality Key" - Brian Muraresku & Graham Hancock

Vitamins & Supplement Recommendations (Please Do Your Research And Consult With Your Doctor First Before Taking Any Vitamins Or Supplements*, This Is What Currently Works For Me And Is Available On Amazon)

- "NATURELO Whole Food Multivitamin for Men" - with Vitamins, Minerals, Organic Herbal Extracts - Vegetarian - for Energy, Brain, Heart, Eye Health
- "Genius Mushroom" - Lions Mane, Cordyceps and Reishi - Immune System Booster & Nootropic Brain Supplement - for Natural Energy, Memory & Liver Support
- "Super Beta Prostate Advanced" (For Men)
- Probiotic of your choice
- 100mg & 200mg Caffeine Pills - since I try not to drink multiple cups of coffee or matcha tea per day with my diabetes to limit the sugar intake while receiving energy boosts as needed.
- "Metagenics Vitamin D3 5,000 IU" - Vitamin D Supplement for Healthy Bone Formation, Cardiovascular Health, and Immune Support

- "Stamiron Tongkat Ali 1000mg Fadogia Agrestis 1000mg Maca 1000mg Turkesterone Extract Supplement" with Ginseng Ashwagandha Fenugreek DAA Saw Palmetto DHEA Nettle

- "Luna" - Naturally Sourced Ingredients | Non-Habit Forming Vegan Capsules | Herbal Supplement with Melatonin, Valerian Root, and more (because sleep is essential to life)

- Apple Cider Vinegar - Can Purchase At Supermarket (they also have flavored versions and capsules now that make it easier to take without mixing in water).

Made in United States
Orlando, FL
14 December 2023